A *Biblical*

HOME EDUCATION

A *Biblical* HOME EDUCATION

BUILDING YOUR HOMESCHOOL ON THE FOUNDATION OF GOD'S WORD

Ruth Beechick

B&H
PUBLISHING GROUP

Nashville, Tennessee

ISBN: 978-0-8054-4454-4

Published by B&H Publishing Group,
Nashville, Tennessee

Dewey Decimal Classification: 371.042
Subject Heading: HOME SCHOOLING

Unless otherwise stated, all Scripture is from
The King James Bible.

1 2 3 4 5 6 7 8   10 09 08 07

CONTENTS

Teaching Helps   ix

Introduction   1

1. Bible for Homeschoolers   5

   Important Bible Doctrines   7

   The Bible as Literature   11

   How the Bible Came to Us   18

   The Main Textbook   20

2. World History to Match the Bible   23

   Early Times   25

   Kingdom of Israel   29

   Gentile Kingdoms   32

   Dating Problems   35

   History Study Materials   36

   Resist the Hype   39

3. Science to Match the Bible   41

   Textbook Problems   42

   The Long Roots of Science   44

   Something for Everybody   47

   Creation Science   48

	National Science Education Standards	52
	Through the Grades	54
4.	Worldviews to Match the Bible	59
	Bible Only	59
	Evolution and Young Earth	61
	Religions	65
	Government and Politics	71
	Family and Society	74
5.	Thinking Skills	77
	Family Thinking Activities	79
	Propaganda	81
	Humors and IQs and Styles	84
	Heart Thinking	89
	Curriculum for Thinking?	92
6.	Reading Skills	95
	Individual Tutoring	98
	Consonants and Vowels	100
	Purpose for Reading	102
	Speed-Reading	104
	Follow-Up	105
	Reading Problems	109
7.	Study Skills	111
	Managing the Study Environment	112
	Dictionary and Reference Skills	115
	Textbook Reading Skills	118
	More Reading Skills	121
	Memory Skills	125
8.	Writing Skills	131
	Writing to Learn	136
	Family Methods	138
	Essays	141

9. Grammar after Writing 147
   How Did Grammar Come to Us? 147
   What Does Grammar Do for Writing? 149
   Prescription or Description? 151
   The Ear Approach 151
   Grammar Last 153
10. Informal Beginnings 157
    Natural Learning 158
    The Immersion Method 162
    Art 165
    Music 168
    Memorizing 169
    Pre-Reading 171
11. Curriculum Materials 175
    Where Curriculums Come From 175
    Labels 177
    Language Skills versus Content Subjects 182
    Ancient Languages 183
    Shopping for Curriculum 184
    Scheduling 194

Appendix: Crossed-Dominance Problems 197
Notes 207
Index 211

TEACHING HELPS

BIBLE

1. Bible Doctrines Listing   11
2. Bible Literature Assignments   17
3. Bible Words Wall Chart   18

WORLD HISTORY

4. Chain-of-Writers Project   28
5. Readings Checklist   28
6. Noah's Ark Model   29
7. Israel Chart   31
8. Tabernacle Model   31
9. Gentile Kingdoms Chart   34
10. Gentile History—A Sweep Through   34

SCIENCE

11. Science Book and Project List   58

WORLDVIEWS

12. Evolution and Young Earth Checklist   65
13. Religious Checklist   70
14. Government Topics Checklist   73
15. Family and Society Checklist   75

THINKING

16. Family Thinking   84

READING

17. Tutoring Plan   98
18. Follow-up Checklist   108

STUDY SKILLS

19. Study Environment Checklist   114
20. Alphabetizing Lessons   115
21. Reference Skills Checklist   118
22. Reading Skills Checklist   124
23. Whole Memory Steps   127
24. Memory Passages Checklist   130

WRITING

25. Writing Ideas Checklist   145

BEGINNINGS

26. Memory Checklist   170
27. Spiritual Development Checklist   173

CURRICULUMS

28. Money-saving Shopping Tip   194

Introduction

Christian homeschoolers are the greatest strength of our churches and our society. Individual hard-working families may feel isolated, but the big picture is that collectively they form a movement of millions that will turn our country back to the Bible, if anybody can do it these days.

Teaching children at home does not have to be as difficult as people make it by trying to follow too much of the world's schooling system that has developed layer upon layer over the years. We can peel away excess layers by the one great principle of viewing language learning as different from the content subjects. Language includes speaking, reading, writing, listening, and thinking. These are *skills* to use for learning Bible and all other content. Children improve these skills by *using* them in their content subjects. That is more effective and more efficient than adding layers of skill classes.

In the first four chapters here we examine some *content subjects* and how each should be closely related to the Bible. Public schooling today has pulled these apart from the Bible. It banishes every thought of God working in the world or of God making the world. Since the fear of the Lord is the beginning of wisdom, that anti-God teaching can lead only to foolishness.

These content chapters provide an overview—the big picture—of curriculum areas, particularly from a biblical perspective. With the big picture, you will be better able to choose curriculum materials and to guide your children through little parts of the picture. You often can connect their learning with the Bible and help them build up their own big picture of God and His creation.

Ancient world history receives more emphasis here because there already are numerous excellent books on the Christian history of America. But we have great need to match ancient history with the Bible, and only a few scholars are working on that. Some young homeschoolers could join them if we open their minds to this fascinating field.

If your children are in public school, these first four chapters can help show areas where you can counteract anti-God views your children learn in school. If you are already homeschooling, these chapters can remind you of why you took your children out of the public system. And they give information on how to stay on the Christian path and not be lured back toward the methods and content of the system you once rejected.

Following the chapters on content are several chapters on *language skills*. These provide insights on efficient ways for children to develop these skills by using them in real life and in the content subjects. They show where to delete most of the separate study and out-of-context drill for these skills. They show probably the greatest time saver and frustration saver of all, and that is to delay grammar until the right time. How to do this and why are laid out in these sections.

Next is a chapter specifically on beginning with young children in a gentle, commonsense manner. The final chapter gives pointers on what kinds of curriculum to buy and, more important, what not to buy.

Strong Christian families build a strong society. The Bible at the center will keep our light shining in a darkening world. While we work hard, we can sing that great line: I read the end of the Book, and we win.

1 Bible for Homeschoolers

The Bible dominates all other books in our Western civilization. Researcher E. D. Hirsch, Jr. wrote, "No one in the English speaking world can be considered literate without a basic knowledge of the Bible."[1] He came to that conclusion after he and colleagues researched a wide range of common reading material to determine what knowledge people need in order to read with good understanding. If someone is said to see the handwriting on the wall or to be meeting Goliath, a reader must know something of the original stories to comprehend the meaning intended. The researchers listed references to all kinds of literature as well as to history, science, politics, arts—anything that is mentioned in reading materials. In the thousands of items collected, the Bible references far outnumbered everything else. So children must learn this book above all others to be educated and literate.

Former literature professor Northrop Frye of Toronto University, though seemingly not a Christian believer, wrote that the Bible "should be taught so early and so thoroughly that it sinks straight to the bottom of the mind, where everything that comes along later can settle on it."[2]

More important than literacy is good moral and spiritual living. The major aim of government schooling is to raise good citizens, good people, so the Bible should be the book for that. But the Bible and its teachings have been removed from public education and that causes trouble in our society. Homeschoolers today are leading a movement back to the Bible. This education is superior intellectually, morally, and spiritually.

A good and free Bible study help is the Online Bible.[3] With this, learn first how to search for English words and phrases. Learn next how to find definitions of Greek and Hebrew words, and then how to search for one of those Greek or Hebrew words—no matter how it is translated in the English. Many other great features are available also. This was an early program offered freely on a ministry basis, and it was so good that it became the model for others now produced commercially. You can download this free or order a CD for a small charge.

For young children you can read from Bible storybooks. During elementary years, phase into using the Bible itself most of the time. It is the primary source. You may find some homeschool curriculum plans that lead you to study the Bible itself, but avoid curriculums that are similar to what your children already have in Sunday school. Those may focus on things that are safe to market to many denominations. The large publishers asked denominational representatives to read each course, and if they found anything that did not strictly fit their church beliefs, it was removed. The end result, then, is a minimized, watered-down curriculum. It lacks the important Bible doctrines. The books also may be ineffective fill-in-the-blank style and filled with trendy teaching theories and padded with twaddle (a wonderful homeschool word) rather than with solid Bible learning.

When you want to teach any particular Bible topic, try a real book by an expert on that topic. Many adult books today are not that hard for children to read. At least read and talk about parts, perhaps parts that answer particular questions. Then the book goes on a shelf alongside your Bibles. It joins your family's permanent collection and is available for future reference, with your under- lining and highlighting to help.

Chronological order does not help during the early years. Children can gather stories and information into their heads in any order, along with memorized passages. After a good background of information, sometime during the teen years, they could do a survey unit to get the big picture of historical order.

The following sections show some reasons why the Bible is important to children's education, and they give suggestions for incorporating it in homeschooling.

Important Bible Doctrines

Your children's worldview and their thinking about every subject are based on their knowledge of Bible doctrines. *Doctrine* means sound, unchanging, and unchangeable teaching based on the Word of God. See if your pastor can give you a good list of doctrines that are important in your church. You need more than a simple statement of salvation and the ordinances of baptism and the Lord's Supper that are sometimes available for guests or prospective members. The list below will work for most serious Bible believing churches. The Scriptures suggested provide a start for teaching the doctrines, and you can add more topics and more Scripture as you wish.

God. Existed eternally; is one God revealed in three persons —Father, Son, and Holy Spirit; created all things in heaven and earth in six days; controls all things. When your children know that God is a Trinity, they can see on this alone that other religions are false.

- ▢ Creator—Genesis 1:1; Exodus 20:11
- ▢ One God—Isaiah 44:6, 8
- ▢ Trinity—John 1:1, 14; Acts 5:3–4; Philippians 1:2

Bible. God's revelation to mankind; each and every word inspired by the Holy Spirit; authoritative; infallible.

- ▢ Deuteronomy 4:2
- ▢ Romans 3:4a
- ▢ 2 Timothy 3:16
- ▢ Revelation 22:18–19
- ▢ Story in Jeremiah 36:10, 21–32

Angels. Mission and activity of the faithful angels and the fallen angels, especially Satan. There is much open talk about ghosts, "aliens" from other planets, and other paranormal phenomena. Don't spend time studying that stuff; but when your children hear some of it, they must be able to relate it to Bible teachings about demons and angels as the "extraterrestrial" beings so as not to believe other strange theories that abound today.

- ▢ Daniel 6:21–22; 8:15–17; Revelation 7:1–4
- ▢ Cherubim and Seraphim—Genesis 3:24; Isaiah 6:1–3; Ezekiel 1:1–25
- ▢ Demons—Luke 9:37–42; 10:1, 17; 2 Peter 2:4
- ▢ Satan—Job 1:6–7 and the story following; Isaiah 14:12–15; John 8:44; 2 Corinthians 11:14; Ephesians 2:2

Man. Created in the image of God; now sinful; must repent and be saved by grace through faith in Christ; the redeemed go to Heaven and the lost go to Hell. Sin affects all mankind and it is the cause of crimes, wars, political oppression, and all evils in the world, though people often blame God. People mishandle these problems because they have false views such as that there is good in every man.

- Created—Genesis 1:27
- Fell into sin—Genesis 3; Romans 3:10
- Needs salvation—Romans 10:9–10; Ephesians 2:8
- Goes to Heaven or Hell—Matthew 7:13–14; John 14:2; Revelation 21:8

Jesus Christ. Existed eternally; appeared in the Old Testament; was born of a virgin to become God in the flesh; died and rose again for our salvation; all things will be gathered in Him in the future. By this one doctrine students can judge the truth or falsity of modern religious talk. Many people have a "Jesus," but it may not be the true Jesus of the Bible.

- John 1:1, 14
- John 8:58 with Exodus 3:14
- Philippians 2:5–8
- Hebrews 1:8
- False christs—Matthew 24:5

Church. One body with Christ as head; for fellowship of believers and for reaching out to the lost. The true Church, some-times called the invisible Church, is made up of believers who are already one in Christ, as He prayed they would be. Visible churches may have some unbelievers in them. Powerful movements today are watering down doctrine and omitting doctrine in order to join all together and build a worldly super-church.

- Should teach *all* true doctrine to all the world— Matthew 28:19–20; Acts 20:27
- Should assemble—Hebrews 10:24–25
- Encourage one another—Colossians 3:16
- Beware of false doctrine—Matthew 16:12; Romans 16:17–18
- Church's foundation—Ephesians 2:19–22
- Made holy—Ephesians 5:26–27
- New Testament letters often instruct churches and their pastors. In Revelation 2 and 3 Christ admonishes the churches.

Future. Rapture, tribulation, antichrist, Second Coming of Christ, millennium, new Heaven and new Earth. (Churches can differ more on future events than elsewhere, because prophecy is not entirely clear until it is fulfilled.) Today's secular talk is filled with jumbled ideas about end times, antichrist, mark of the beast, and other Bible matters that people know only vaguely. Children need the Bible teachings.

- Luke 21:25–27
- 1 Thessalonians 4:16–17
- Revelation 4 to 22

Study of Bible doctrines, its unchangeable teachings, is called theology. Theology used to be called the queen of the sciences because all other learnings were unified in this biblical worldview. Scholarship in all fields is integrated and becomes one within

Bible theology; nothing else can so unify. Christian homeschoolers are leading a movement to crown the queen again.

Teaching Suggestions

Use the list above or keep your church's doctrine list in your teacher notebook or other handy place. Periodically choose a topic and use some of the related Scriptures to teach it. Your students could search for more information on Internet or in books on your Bible reference shelf, or buy a new book—a real book—for the occasion.

The Bible as Literature

Besides doctrine, the Bible is good for study of worldviews, history, and science, and those are treated in separate chapters. Here we focus on the literary aspects of the Bible. If we know, for instance, what is poetry and what is narrative, that is crucial to properly understanding a passage. This knowledge also carries over to other literature and strengthens other learning as well.

Professor Frye knew all kinds of literature from throughout all of history better than just about anybody. He wrote that he found no other book in the world with a structure even remotely like that of the Christian Bible. The Bible does not match any genre of writing that he knew. Its history is not like our history books that try to give evidence and arguments to convince the reader. Biography likewise. Its description and narrative are not like ours that tell what we would see if we were there; they tell what we *should* see. Its poetry transcends ours in profound ways, and much of its prose uses condensed and concrete language like our poetry. The Bible does not fit into the style of writing of any historical period.

In short, there is no way to categorize the Bible by traditional literary categories. Frye adopted a word to use for the Bible alone—proclamation.[4] It is a category by itself. Here are some of the literary characteristics of the Bible.

Metaphors. Metaphors are more than frivolous ornaments of poetry or of flowery prose. In the Bible, metaphor controls much of the meaning. Joseph is a fruitful bough. Judah is a lion's whelp (cub). Shepherd, sheep, and flock; bride, bridegroom, and wedding; sowing and harvesting; good seed and bad seed; and numerous other items fill the Bible with *images* for metaphorical thinking.

Often the word *is* is not included, as when Jesus called Herod a fox. English courses spend time identifying whether something is a metaphor like the Herod-fox or a simile that Herod *is like* a fox. Either way, the important aspect is that your children learn the metaphorical mode of thinking.

In general, what we call metaphors are those that occur together in time. Herod and foxes lived simultaneously. Farmer's seed and the seed of the Word exist simultaneously.

Types. Types, in contrast to metaphors, are separated by time. The Flood, according to Jesus, is a *type* of a future destruction. The Flood was an actual event that foreshadows its *antitype,* an actual event that comes later in history. In some cases the antitype has already happened and in other cases it is yet future. So this literary form is found in both history and prophecy.

God bringing His people out of Egypt is a type of His bringing us out of the slavery of sin. Noah's ark of safety is a type of

Christ providing our safety in salvation. The tabernacle in the wilderness points to Christ in so many ways that whole books are written about it. The antitype is always greater than the type that foreshadows it. Old Testament writers did not treat the events as types, but New Testament writers refer back to the events and treat them as types. Extrabiblical writers often do the same, as crossing the Jordan into the promised land is used in hymns and elsewhere to picture our crossing into Heaven at death.

With young children, teach the stories themselves. This gives the background that they need to understand them as types when they are old enough—beginning about fourth grade and later.

Talk about types with your children so they learn to think biblically in this way. This important kind of thinking led to the theory that there is meaning and purpose in history. Even evolutionists, whose theory rests on random chance, try to say that evolution is going somewhere. Professor Frye said that this confidence in historical process is a legacy of biblical typology.[5] He knew of no other possible source.

Parables. Parables are another use of metaphor—analogy—in the Bible. As with types, teach the stories to young children, and at about fourth grade they can begin to understand the analogies in them.

Research on children's thinking of analogy shows that full understanding arrives gradually.[6] At first children can see analogies of actions: the potter *makes* the pot and God *makes* us. Second, children can understand analogies of actors: the *potter* makes something and *God* makes something. Third, are the objects: the potter makes the *pot* and God makes *us*. It usually requires further mental development for children to understand analogies of objects such as the *pot* and *us* in this example. In this parable the pot can be the child himself and that makes it easier than if the pot stood for something else.

Use the above information loosely. That is, you need not have separate lessons at different ages for actions, actors, and objects acted upon. And you need not quiz children on details of analogies. Teach whole stories without tearing them apart too much. Explain the metaphoric matters and let children's understanding grow gradually.

Hebrew poetry. A feature of much Hebrew poetry is *couplets.* Couplets are two lines that say the same thing but say it in different ways. Here is a clear illustration from Psalm 19:1–2.

> *The heavens declare the glory of God;*
> *and the firmament showeth his handiwork.*
> *Day unto day uttereth speech,*
> *and night unto night showeth knowledge.*

In verse 1 the heavens and the firmament, two names for the same thing, both show attributes of God. This is stated in two ways. In verse 2 the ongoing days and nights both reveal information. This is parallel construction. Look at this outline of parallelism from verses 7 and 8 of Psalm 19.

> *law is perfect, testimony is sure.*
> *statutes right, commandment pure.*

Each of those four statements has a good result, so that carries the parallelism further yet. Here are the full lines as translated in the King James Bible.

> *The law of the LORD is perfect, converting the soul:*
> *The testimony of the LORD is sure, making wise the simple.*

> *The statutes of the LORD are right, rejoicing the heart:*
> *The commandment of the LORD is pure, enlightening the eyes.*

Sometimes couplets extend into triplets. Sometimes the parallel features are reversed. For this reversed form the last phrase of verse 8 above would read: *The eyes are enlightened, from the pure commandment of the Lord.* For good examples of reversed couplets see verses 2 and 3 and verses 4 and 5 of Psalm 113.

You can see there are not rigid couplet rules, but your children from about fifth grade and up can enjoy noticing patterns in Bible poems.

New Testament writers writing Greek prose also sometimes used the couplet pattern. This example from 1 Corinthians 12:17 requires metaphorical thinking, since the physical body with eyes and ears stands for the body of Christ with its various parts.

If the whole body were an eye, where were the hearing?
If the whole were hearing, where were the smelling?

Another feature that Hebrew poetry sometimes uses is *acrostic*. Psalm 34 has twenty-two verses and each verse begins with a letter of the Hebrew alphabet—in order. That simplified the memorizing for Hebrew children.

Knowing what is poetry in the Bible helps us to figure out the meaning of a passage. People sometimes think that poetry is a high flight of fancy words without specific meaning, with just a general emotional effect. Some people interpret Genesis 1 that way. If they do not want to take this creation story literally as a narrative, they say it is "mere" poetry. By that they mean that we cannot really understand it; we can only see somebody waxing flowery over creation. Those people cannot tell the difference between prose and poetry. But your children can learn to tell the difference. In Genesis 1 we read straightforward narrative. Examples:

God said, Let there be light
God called the light Day

let the dry land appear
the evening and the morning were the third day

That chapter contains no indication of poetic features. Compare the lines above with these poetic lines about creation from Psalms 24 and 104.

For he hath founded it upon the seas,
and established it upon the floods.

who stretcheth out the heavens like a curtain . . .
who walketh upon the wings of the wind

The first lines here you will recognize as a couplet. The last two are rich with metaphoric imagery. As careful readers we should be able to decide that these examples are poetic and the Genesis 1 example is narrative. Research on the poem versus narrative forms is described in the next chapter.

Metaphorical thinking. All the above elements of literature require metaphorical thinking. Images, metaphors, similes, types, parables, poetry and other parallel couplets—also proverbs, epigrams, and still other elements of Bible writing—use metaphor. The Bible is more packed with metaphor than any other book in the world. Other writing is full of it too, more so the older literature than current literature. Poetry is built on metaphor. All arts use it. The concrete language of metaphor began in the most ancient times we know of and has lived through the ages.

Metaphorical thinking differs from logic. In logic *A* is not *B;* Joseph is not a bough. But in metaphor *A* is said to be *B;* Joseph *is* a bough. You can insert *is like* a bough if it helps, but metaphor is not a little word game for writers to play; it is a powerful mode of thinking. It uses concrete images, pictures that we can visualize in our heads, rather than abstractions as logic does.

It is important for your children to become acquainted with Bible metaphors and poems. These are not artsy decorations to their learning; they are necessary for clear thinking about doctrine and history and other weighty matters of Bible knowledge. The best way to teach this is bit-by-bit, on-the-spot attention to metaphoric elements when you run into them in family Bible reading, children's memory verses, or home review of Sunday school or other lessons. Occasionally you can expand on this incidental approach by assignments such as these:

Teaching Suggestions

1. Choose examples from this section, look them up in the Bible, about one per day, and talk about the metaphor or couplet or other feature in the example. (The KJV works best for this.)

2. After you read something in the Bible, write labels in the margins for couplet, type, parable, metaphor, or other literary feature.

3. Write out a poetic Bible passage with lines to look like our English poems. Some translations already do this, but their narrow columns may hinder.

4. Try writing one or more couplets. Use your own topic, or use a praise or other topic you find in the psalms.

5. Try writing an acrostic. The first line begins with *A,* the second begins with *B* and so forth. Or the beginning letters could form a word such as *Paul,* or your own name. Or write in couplets, the first two lines beginning with the first letter, the next two beginning with the second letter, and so forth.

These assignments provide language and literature learning, so you can skip other language work on days you use these.

Vocabulary. The most sensible place to expand children's vocabulary is in their literature and other content subjects. Your children will meet important words in the Bible that are not likely to be taught in any vocabulary course—big words like omnipotent, regeneration, Godhead, and justification; and smaller words like devils and hell. Children should learn these one by one as they read and talk about the Bible. Do not wait for a reading curriculum or vocabulary curriculum to teach them.

Teaching Suggestion

As your children learn new Bible words, add them to a wall chart so they are available for review and for use in conversing or writing.

How the Bible Came to Us

Here is a short history of how our English Bible came to us. The original letters and histories of the New Testament that Paul and others wrote were copied and recopied and carried around to the churches. Other writers, too, wrote for the church, and church leaders agreed on which writings were part of the "canon" to be added to the Hebrew Scriptures and which were not. When the King James translators went to work, they had more than 5000 manuscripts of the New Testament that agreed with each other. These manuscripts are called the Received Text, or *Textus Receptus* in Latin. God had promised to preserve His Word for all generations (Psalm 12:6–7) and this seems a better way to do it than to have one original copy in a church or museum somewhere that people claimed was the "original." Who can question 5000-plus copies that say the same thing? For the Old Testament, the translators used the Masoretic text, the one carefully handed down from generation to generation by the Jews.

The King James translators numbered almost fifty who were able to continue for the whole seven years of work. The scholars were divided into six teams assigned to six portions of the Bible. Each man separately translated every word of his team's portion. Then the team met and hashed out any differences. Then each team passed their work to the other five teams for further examination and approval. This Bible spread around the English speaking world and has been widely used ever since.

While all that was going on, other people were trying to tear down God's Word. Back in the third century some Jews were teaching and studying in Greek schools in Alexandria, Egypt, and the Bible there was becoming corrupt. Jews there made a Greek version of the Hebrew Old Testament that we now call the Septuagint. They made a New Testament, too. One famous writer there was Origen. He did not believe in Hell, the deity of Christ, His atonement for sin, Bible infallibility, and many other important doctrines. After he died, his writings were passed on to historian Eusebius.

Emperor Constantine asked Eusebius for fifty copies of the Bible to send to fifty cities, so he used Origen's writings to make those for the emperor. The churches of that day did not *receive* that heretical version. They did not use it or make copies of it, and it almost became lost to history. Then in the 1800s two manuscripts were found that could possibly be two of those fifty, one found in the Vatican and one in a monastery in the Sinai. Those two were not complete and they had many differences between them. Yet a couple of men (Brooke Westcott and Fenton J. A. Hort) made a Greek New Testament from those two manuscripts. These men, like Origen, did not believe in many essential Christian doctrines. They said the Vaticanus and Sinaiticus manuscripts were older and better than the over 5000 manuscripts of the *Textus Receptus* (also called *Majority Text*). We might ask whether God's true Word was lost for those many centuries until somebody found it again, or did God preserve it for all those generations through the *Majority Text?* Most new English versions today come from the Greek New Testament begun by Origen.[7]

Some new Bibles claim to be more readable, but the Flesch readability formula and others, too, show that they are not. Some claim to be in the "people's" language, but the King James translators deliberately wrote in a higher language meant to be timeless, and not in the everyday language of their times. They handled delicate matters delicately and did not descend to street language. The King James Bible has been read by more people than any other Bible in history. Educated students in the English speaking world must know it.

The Main Textbook

Homeschoolers who try to do everything that advertisers and others say they need soon find themselves overloaded, so they must look for ways to simplify the curriculum. This book suggests a number of ways to do that. Start by using the Bible as the main textbook. It leads your children to eternal salvation and leads them to making good use of their lives while here on earth. Beyond that, it leads to a better academic education than the humanist and pagan and other approaches the world uses.

This chapter has pointed out that knowing Bible doctrine is the basis of right thinking on all subjects. It has shown that students can get an excellent literary education by using the Bible, as well as excellent training in thinking. So the topics here can substitute for some of your other curriculum on literature and writing skills and thinking skills. This is the key to simplifying homeschooling: Practice language skills in the content subjects and not in isolation separately in a language course. Remember that language skills include thinking as well as reading and writing.

Further in this book we will examine worldview learning, science learning, and other learnings that need to be based on the Bible. The Bible is the main textbook for your Christian home-school. It is the greatest book the world has ever known, the classic of all classics. Our students, and we too, should study it to show ourselves approved unto God (2 Timothy 2:15).

2 World History to Match the Bible

G od is the author and controller of history. So to get it right we must match history with the Bible—not only its time line and chronology, but also the principles and the meanings we attach to it. Secular history books do neither. The chronology is wrong and the meanings are wrong unless we use the Bible and books by Bible believing writers.

One false view is the evolutionary; this affects history as well as science. Evolutionists believe that man took a long time to develop language and agriculture, but in the Bible Adam talked and farmed at the beginning. And immediately after the Flood Noah did too. Another false view of history is the "scientific" view in which historians try to discover laws of cause and effect. They try to find patterns for things like why nations fall or how leaders rise to power. But history does not work like science. Laws should help people predict events, as the law of gravity predicts that a ball will fall if you drop it, and history is not predictable that way. Thus it is false to consider it scientific.

Bible believers see that God sets up kings and brings them down. God's history is going somewhere. This contrasts with pagan religions that see history as cyclical, one cycle following another, round and round, going nowhere in particular. Christianity views history as linear, proceeding in a line toward a predetermined end. Only the Christian view includes the plan and purpose that God is working out. He chose a nation to bring the Bible and the Savior to mankind. He helps Christians to fight Satan's evil forces. The Bible tells about this war, the conflict that *produces* history in the world. Christians are the only ones who understand that conflict, who see this good-versus-evil principle working in the world while events move toward the Kingdom of Christ. We may not understand everything along the way but we trust the God of history. We may not know all the details but we know the big plan of history revealed in the Bible.

This chapter sweeps through that big plan, giving an overall picture. It is good to start with the big picture rather than getting lost in details. Begin by seeing three major periods of history that the Bible shows. Children can easily learn them. This simple three-part outline can help older students pull together into organized form the history knowledge they already have. Children without much background yet can learn to fit future learnings into the periods where they belong. The brief outline looks like this.

1. Early Times
2. Kingdom of Israel
3. Gentile Kingdoms

Those three periods carry you all the way from creation to Christ's Kingdom. Following are some ideas for learning about these periods in your homeschool. First, a look at Early Times.

Early Times

Genesis contains the oldest writings in the world. Not long ago historians thought that Moses could not have written the books of Moses because writing had not been invented yet in Moses' time. Well, historians dug up more ancient ruins and discovered that, sure enough, Moses could have written. Then they discovered very ancient Sumerian stories of the Flood, written before Moses' time. So now they believe that Moses copied from the Sumerians.

From the Bible we learn the true sequence. Noah and his sons were eyewitnesses, and they wrote the original true story of the Flood. In a moment we will see evidence for that. Noah's writings, along with Adam's and other early writers, were passed down from son to son. Like most ancient writings, we do not have the originals. If they were written on stone, they could be preserved somewhere. Some explorers hope to find Noah's tomb and hope they will find his manuscripts buried there with him. Many historians would be shocked. They would have to change their theory once again. They will have to say that Noah wrote the story first and the Sumerians copied his—with many errors and pagan changes.

Without waiting for the slow historians, we can see from the Bible that the early manuscripts were passed down and finally reached Moses. He compiled the ancient writings and organized them into what we call the book of Genesis. Jesus and several New Testament writers quote from and refer to Genesis often, but never once do they say these are the words of Moses. When they refer to Exodus, Leviticus, Numbers, or Deuteronomy, they call those the words of Moses. But not Genesis. The Genesis events were ancient history to Moses, but events in the other four books happened in his time. He was eyewitness and the original writer of those.

Clues in Genesis itself show us who wrote that early history. Some are language clues. For instance, Abraham and Isaac used Egyptian words that fit the Old Kingdom of Egypt but do not fit the Middle Kingdom of Moses' time. Moses did not change those words when he compiled Genesis. Another clue is place names. The original writers used the names of their own times, of course. Editor Moses left the original names, but when necessary he added the current name so readers of his time would know where it was. Example: Bela, which is Zoar.

Another clue is how each ancient book included in Genesis is "signed off" by its writer or writers. These sign-offs are listed below. After the list are instructions for children to show in their Bibles this "chain" of writers.

1. Genesis 2:4: *These are the generations* [beginnings] *of the heavens and of the earth when they were created.* This does not quite say I, God, wrote this, but He was the eyewitness who could write it. God must have written it for Adam so he would have the true story of creation to pass down to his children. Throughout this account God is called "God" (*Elohim,* the three-in-one).

2. Genesis 5:1: *This is the book of the generations of Adam.* This tells about the garden of Eden and of Cain killing Abel. Adam was there and could write of his own times. He called God "Lord God." This difference indicates that it is a different writer now in the second book.

3. Genesis 6:9: *These are the generations of Noah.* Noah wrote a short book about the wickedness in the earth (or maybe Moses included only a short part of Noah's writings). About himself, Noah wrote only that he found grace in the eyes of the Lord.

4. Genesis 10:1: *Now these are the generations of the sons of Noah, Shem, Ham, and Japheth.* The sons told what

a good man Noah was. And they wrote details of the Flood year, as well as of the rainbow and a few happenings afterward.

5. Genesis 11:27: *Now these are the generations of Terah.* Terah was Abraham's father. His book contains only a list of who begat whom from the Flood down to himself. He must have inherited that family list of births that passed down each generation until it came to him.

6. Genesis 25:19: *And these are the generations of Isaac, Abraham's son.* This ends a long book that probably both Abraham and Isaac wrote telling their adventures. Isaac evidently included some information from his half-brother Ishmael. That is introduced with the signature in verse 12: *Now these are the generations of Ishmael, Abraham's son.* This book just names Ishmael's sons and tells where they lived.

7. Genesis 37:2: *These are the generations of Jacob.* Jacob wrote about working for Laban to win his bride Rachel. Embedded within this book are two sections by his twin brother Esau. Those little books are introduced in 36:1 and 9. Both times the signature says *These are the generations of Esau.* Esau names his sons and grandsons and tells how they moved to Edom (now Jordan).

8. Exodus 1:1: *Now these are the names of the children of Israel.* This signature formula is slightly changed from the others, not using the word "generations." The sons of Israel (Jacob) were Joseph and his eleven brothers. They wrote about the famine at home as well as happenings in Egypt—how Joseph rose to power and how the whole family moved there. They knew and wrote about details of Egyptian life in early times that Moses would not have known in his time four generations later. This is

evidence that Joseph and some of his brothers wrote this last book in Genesis.

Chain-of-Writers Project

Your children can find the writers' signatures readily in their Bibles without having to learn the references. They only need to learn to start at Genesis 2:4. To mark this "chain" of writers they begin by finding the signature in Genesis 2:4 and underlining part of it, just the words "generations of," or more if they like. In the margin write the next reference—Genesis 5:1. Turn to Genesis 5:1 and repeat the procedure of underlining and writing the next reference. Books 6 and 7 have embedded books, and they can omit those or figure out some way to note them in the margin along with the main signature. When the chain is completed the children will be able to show who wrote all the books just by remembering to begin at Genesis 2:4. Let them show this to your adult visitors; they probably never heard it before.

This project will be more meaningful to children after they know stories about some major characters in Genesis—Adam, Noah, Abraham, Isaac, Jacob, and Joseph.

Checklist of Readings

- ⊠ Genesis 1 to 11   _____
- ⊠ *Adam and His Kin*[1]   _____
- ⊠ Books about creation (list each)
- ⊠ Books about the Flood (list each)

Activity

- Model of Noah's ark[2]

Kingdom of Israel

Roots of our western civilization go back to Israel, and not only to Greece and Rome as history books so often teach. The Greek roots are pagan and the Israel roots are biblical. So Christian homeschoolers spend much time learning the Bible.

The Bible is the best source for teaching about Israel, as it was for teaching the Early Times. The Israel period begins with "father" Abraham in the book of Genesis and continues through Moses and Joshua, then through Kings and Chronicles, ending with the final fall of Judah. Some prophets belong here also. Bible storybooks can help for reading about many of these events. The fall of Judah marks the beginning of the Gentile period that follows.

The chart on the next page shows the major sweep of the history of Israel.

The history of Israel is closely intertwined with Egypt, and children can merge the two instead of keeping Israel in their Sunday school file and Egypt in their school file. Abraham and Lot visited Egypt during its Old Kingdom. It was not desert then, but was like "the garden of the Lord" before God rained brimstone and fire from heaven.[3]

Joseph's brothers sold him into Egypt during its Middle Kingdom, and all of his family moved down there during a famine. Later, a new pharaoh enslaved these Israelites and Moses came along to free them. At this exodus the pharaoh and all his army drowned in the Red Sea, and death and destruction hobbled the homeland too. That is how the Middle Kingdom of Egypt collapsed.

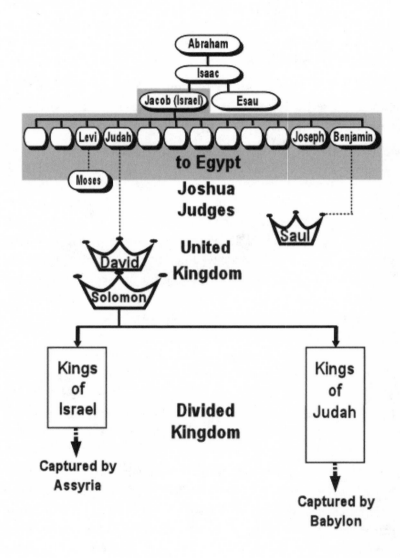

KINGDOM OF ISRAEL

After that, Egyptians disappear from Bible history for a long time. They did not bother Moses anymore, and they never warred against Joshua or the judges either. Some foreigners were ruling cruelly over Egypt. Finally the first Israelite king, Saul, helped to oust the foreigners and to put a true pharaoh on the throne again.[4] That is when the New Kingdom of Egypt began. Solomon married an Egyptian princess, and Israel and Egypt had friendly relations for a while.

Israel Chart

Some children may enjoy making a larger, dressed-up version of the Israel chart to display on a wall. If they do, make good use of it by referring to it after a Sunday school lesson or Bible reading on any event or person in Israel's history. Try to determine where it should appear on the chart.

Tabernacle Model

For children who like the handwork of making models, try a model of the tabernacle either from scratch or from a kit.[5] Or sketch a floor plan of the building and courts. An alternative is a temple model or floor plan. A further study is to compare that plan with the plan of Ezekiel's temple vision, which is not in the time of the law but the time of the Lord's glory.[6] These projects take much time and study, but the Bible devotes about fifty chapters to the tabernacle and a good many to the Temple also, so this indicates great importance for these structures.

Gentile Kingdoms

After Israel and Judah fell into captivity, the period of the Gentile kingdoms began. Daniel was a teenager then and was one of the captives in Babylon. One night King Nebuchadnezzar dreamed a dream and only Daniel could interpret it. The dream was of a statue, an image of a man, described in Daniel 2.

This remarkable image shows the whole history of the Gentile world from Babylon through to the kingdom of Christ that will last for ever and ever. Here is a brief description of each part of the image.

Head of gold. Daniel said to Nebuchadnezzar, "You are this head of gold." God had given Nebuchadnezzar that gold kingdom and power and glory. But it would not last forever. The story of Babylon's fall is in Daniel 5. The nation of Babylon today is much smaller and is known as Iraq.

Breast and arms of silver. The silver kingdom followed the gold. At first this was the combined Medo-Persian empire, but Cyrus the Persian soon gained full control. Cyrus let the captive Jews return to their homeland. Some did and some continued to live among the Gentiles. Esther was queen for one of Persia's kings. The nation of Persia today is much smaller and is known as Iran. (Related Scripture: 2 Chronicles 36:22 to Ezra 1:4 and Ezra 2.)

Belly and thighs of brass. The brass kingdom was Greece. Alexander the Great is the famous leader who conquered silver Persia and much more besides. He founded cities named Alexandria all over the place. One of these was in Egypt, and there the Greeks set up a library to collect all the knowledge of the world. They called seventy Jews (tradition says) to translate the Old Testament into Greek. That translation, called the *Septuagint,* still exists but many say it is not an accurate translation from the original *Masoretic* Hebrew version. Alexander died at a young age and his kingdom broke into four parts, as Daniel had said it would (11:3–4). Greece now is confined to a peninsula and some islands in southern Europe.

Legs of iron. The mighty iron empire was Rome. When Caesar Augustus came to power he ended the republican form of government and gathered all political power to himself. His empire included the land of Israel, and during his reign Jesus was born there (Luke 2:1–20). This was the longest lasting and largest of the empires on the image. The two legs might be showing that the Roman Empire would break into two parts—the Eastern and Western.

Feet of iron and clay. The Roman Empire broke into pieces. The iron pieces in the feet and toes show that the strength of Rome remains in parts while clay is mixed in. Daniel said the kingdom would subdue all things, break them in pieces and bruise (Daniel 2:40). That is exactly what the European parts of the empire did. They conquered and bruised most of the world. They ruled over far-flung colonies for one thousand years—from about 900 to the 1900s. Iron and clay pieces were everywhere.

At the Yalta Conference during World War II, the Allied leaders made plans for the European nations to give up their empires. So for the next fifty years, almost up to the year 2000, nation after nation around the world became independent. One of the first nations was Israel, formed in 1948.

To read the Bible on Israel rising again, leave Daniel's image for a moment and go to the words of Jesus. He said that when the fig tree (Israel) and all the trees (many nations) begin to sprout their leaves, then summer is near. He said to look up because our redemption is very near (Luke 21:29–31).

In the end of Nebuchadnezzar's dream a great stone cut out of the mountain smashed to smithereens the whole image, the iron, the brass, the clay, the silver, and the gold. The stone became a great mountain, and this means the God of Heaven will set up a kingdom to fill the earth.

Chart of Gentile Kingdoms

One person in the family may enjoy drawing a large, colorful picture of the image in Daniel 2. Try to find what an ancient king from Babylon might have been dressed like. Use these labels:

Head of gold—Babylon,

Breast and arms of silver—Persia,

Belly and thighs of brass—Greece,

Legs of iron—Rome,

Feet of iron and clay—broken Roman Empire.

Display the drawing on a wall and use it as a time line. That is, whenever you are reading some history from the Gentile period, have your students decide where on the image it fits.

Sweep through Gentile History

If you wish to teach from this book, for each lesson read the description of one of the five portions of the image. Then read the Scripture given there. You can follow up with discussion, calling to mind various facts your children already know about that period of Gentile history. They should know that Jesus lived in Roman times, and the early church in Acts was still Roman times.

This Gentile period is already more than two thousand years long. In contrast to the Early Times and the Israel period, you will need a wide array of materials rather than mostly the Bible and Bible-oriented materials. Some curriculum shopping helps follow later.

Dating Problems

Homeschoolers have been oversold on the idea that knowing dates equals knowing history. Think for a moment about what exactly a date does for you. Sometimes it helps you feel that you could answer a test question. More importantly, it sometimes helps you figure out the sequence of some events. Who conquered whom? What kingdom followed another?

If the purpose of date learning is to get to the sequence of history events, then we are going at it backwards. We can learn the sequence to start with. That is more meaningful and more interesting to do. That is a major thrust of this chapter: learn the sequence of history. Attach a few dates if you like. A few anchor dates are all that children need to memorize. If they know that Solomon's date was about 1000 BC, then they know that all the kings (except Saul and David) came after that date, and they know that Moses and the judges and everybody before the kings were before that date. See what one anchor date does? Numerous dates are unnecessary.

The current situation is that ancient dates are wrong, anyway—wrong this way in one book and wrong that way in the next book. Some get their dates from the so-called archeological ages of Stone Age, Bronze Age, and so forth. Others use chemical dating, which has numerous problems. The Institute for Creation Research has completed a multi-pronged research on this and published their findings.[7] Most books use dates that are supposed to match with dates from ancient Egypt, but Egypt's dates are now shown to be wrong by several centuries. Many books simply copy from one another. In the midst of this scrambled situation, the homeschool community is obsessed with learning dates. Could it be that this stems from the textbook and testing experience in our own schooling? Today's children can be free from that date obsession, particularly with dates of ancient history. They can learn meaningful history instead, learning the whys and hows more than the exact whens.

For ancient history, all the "scientific" dating systems have problems, so the Bible is the best dating tool. It shows when the world began, when the Flood came, when nations began, and when Egypt's kingdoms began and ended. It clears up the ancient history that is so twisted in secular books.[8]

History Study Materials

A homeschool catalog states that they have 30,000 books. If you do not see what you want in the catalog, then ask for it, it says. Other catalogs help by saying they have already selected some of the best, so you can choose from their selections. Conventions have the best and less than best side by side in scores of booths. Any way you approach it, the shopping task is overwhelming. Give up trying to compare everything. Use your common sense to select something, and then stop worrying about your selections.

The main shopping principle for history and most related topics is that the materials be clearly biblical. This is urgent in the most ancient history because practically all secular books teach the evolutionary view, which distorts history as well as science. You can often spot problems even in brief catalog descriptions. One blurb says the book teaches "10 chronological periods from 40,000 BC to 2003." Another says its book ranges from "Prehistoric Times to the Twentieth Century." That impossibly old date and the term "prehistoric" show that the books are evolutionary and not biblical. Another blurb states that the book begins with the "prehistoric African savanna." This refers to a current "politically correct" theory that civilization began in black Africa, rather than rebuilding in Shinar after the Flood, as the Bible says.

Catalogs from many Christian companies carry also secular, nonbiblical materials. But today there are so many Christian history books that there is no need to buy secular books. When your children do happen to read non-biblical books, help them critique what is wrong with them. We must realize that homeschoolers are now a big market, and big business out there is doing what big business is good at doing. On the other hand, some people are supplying materials with a true ministry motivation. But even some of these seem not aware that teaching a world history of hundreds of thousands of years, or even tens of thousands, is an evolutionary view.

Here are some choices now available.

Regular old-fashioned textbooks. Sometimes beginning home-schoolers feel more comfortable with textbooks because that is what they had in school and they understand how to use them. If this is your case, you might also remember that you were not especially excited about studying history. That is a common result because textbooks do not focus on stories; they skim too rapidly over too many facts. You can begin with a textbook anyway, with the resolve that you will use it loosely as soon as you learn ways to do so. Skip or correct the early world parts that do not match the Bible.

Unit studies. The term "unit studies" describes many Christian history curriculums that provide a basic outline and list of books to read for a unit on each period or topic in the outline. They provide, also, teaching ideas for projects, for writing, and for discussions. Your children, and you too, can learn a lot of history by following one of these plans. You are likely to find that there is too much to cover, and that is OK; you need not cover everything in the curriculum, but use it loosely. Spend more time on the topics that interest your children the most or that you feel are most important. Spend a little time on other topics, too, because some children might discover an interest that way.

It is not important at all to move chronologically through history. This is a great advantage for homeschoolers. It means that all your children can read about one topic at the same time and talk about it with each other. Presenting history in order does not result in children knowing history in order. A better plan is to begin with stories. Then in teen years, after students have built a background of information, they can do a unit that pulls together their history knowledge into sequential order.[8] Using the Daniel image chart also helps to gain a chronological view.

No curriculum, real books only. Some families begin by reading biographies for a while, or battle stories, or pioneer or missionary stories. Any good reading like this is valuable history learning. You can read widely with profit for quite some time. Later you may think, "We should learn more about the Reformation." Then you and the children find a book or two about the Reformation, or whatever event or place you have chosen. This resembles the unit curriculums but you do it yourself. It is surprisingly easy to make your own units with real books. Just begin with no-plan activities like reading a portion aloud and talking about it, or begin with the children reading on their own and telling you what they read. That can lead to more books or to activities. Some books suggest activities and children may suggest others—making maps or charts, learning music or food of a period, and so on. Some books suggest writing assignments, and that is valuable learning for both writing and history. The first unit you try may be rather short, but that's OK. They grow longer and better as the children gain experience.

Some parents get their topic ideas from a broad outline in a textbook or from a scope and sequence chart somewhere. Choosing your own books allows you to pass up those with nonbiblical teachings. This real-book approach has turned on many students to history, whereas the traditional textbook approach turns many off.

Non-book materials. Vendors offer a wide variety of video, audio, and computer materials. You can add these to books in any mixture that you like. Because computers are the newest does not make them more effective. Learning happens in the child's mind, not in the curriculum. Computer games or courses can be dull and trivial like anything else. Or they can be exciting and include rich content. Add museum visits or local historical sites, and try interviewing elderly friends and relatives about their lives.

Resist the Hype

Many school district and government lists of goals try to tell you what to teach, and it usually is an overwhelming amount. The government complicates this more by specifying what to teach in each grade. This plan is useful for standardizing graded schools but is entirely unnecessary for homeschooling.

Hype is shoved at you from all quarters—from the schooling mind-set of society, from the politics of testing, and from curriculum advertisements. All you have to do is get the right content in the right order, they say, and use the correct teaching formulas, and *voila* your children will end up knowing history. Oh yes, you have to diagnose your children's learning styles and your teaching style. You have to plan hands-on activities, and you need visuals. On and on it goes. You can throw out much of this educationese hype about how and what to teach.

If you read the lofty goals the government publishes, do not be intimidated. Too many committee members have contributed too many items. It is impossible even for a history professor to achieve the goals set for high school. One professor said that history is for old people, meaning that it takes that long to build enough wide knowledge and understanding. With curriculum too, the writers inevitably include more than one family can accomplish. They have to be sure that the most serious history buffs have plenty of material, and they allow for different families to choose different activities from among the suggestions. For your own sanity, then, scale back your goals to realistic levels.

One mother whose daughter was not yet school age wrote out years of history lesson plans according to the system of a particular convention speaker. Then she had a new baby, a difficult one, and life changed. They traded school desks for another sofa and embarked on years of relaxed homeschooling using real books and an informal approach. Those two children at college age were doing real world work that many college graduates could not do. Three younger children followed similarly. Real books all the way.

If your children read and learn throughout their schooling years, what more can they do? Listening and watching other media count too. Along the way they could learn some topics with deeper understanding, as this helps them realize how complex might be other topics that they know less well. This is a better state of things than skimming evenly over everything as textbooks tend to do.

So do not sweat the history. As a Christian, especially if you know the Bible, you already have a good grasp of what it is about. Relax and enjoy it with your children. Read and learn together about other times and other places. Compare what the books say with what the Bible says. Keep reading the Bible too. It is the ultimate history book. It gives you the true view of history as working out God's purpose all the way from creation to the new Earth.

3 Science to Match the Bible

The modern science revolution would not have happened without the biblical thinking of great men like Galileo and Isaac Newton. Pagan thinking could not have accomplished what they did. Bertrand Russell, though not a Christian himself, wrote that "Christianity is the mother of science." He understood that the revolution came about through belief in a rational God who would make a unified, orderly universe that man can observe and discover laws of cause and effect.

Homeschooling parents who are not scientists themselves seem to fear science more than any other subject, but it helps to view science as simply learning about God's wonderful creation and praising Him for it. This chapter provides overviews of science topics and explores how and when to teach them. This big picture can help you navigate your way through the territory. This also explains some of the reasons that homeschoolers, particularly Christian homeschoolers, can do better than public schools.

The public schools have not earned an *A* in science teaching, or even a *C*. Goals 2000, with a lot of federal money, had as one goal that our high school graduates would be first in the world in science. But by 2000 they scored nineteenth out of the twenty-one nations that participated in testing. Something is terribly wrong with our school science teaching. A look at the textbook system shows a lot of what is wrong and at the same time indicates what we can do differently.

Textbook Problems

A fifth grade science textbook says that "Crow moon is the name given to spring because that is when the crows return," and it continues for three pages of Algonquin Indian lore before telling that the rotation and tilt of the earth, not crows, affect climate. This politically correct attention to Indians and other minorities pervades the books to an "absurd effect" according to a teacher committee. Books feature Marie Curie with a picture and a half page of text, while her husband Pierre is shown only as a supportive spouse. In actual history, they won a Nobel Prize together and some have said that Pierre Curie probably helped more people than any other scientist has. Edison's small picture appears next to a larger picture of black scientist Lewis Latimer who improved the light bulb that Edison invented. Einstein may not be mentioned at all. That distortion is another feature that the large committee of teachers rated in science textbooks, and they rated it low.

Another fault that caused low ratings was the weakness in teaching important concepts. Books focused, instead, on teaching technical terms and trivial details that are easy to test. Some Christian curriculums fall into that pattern, too, because of beliefs about schooling or simply because of imitating the majors.

A third textbook feature that received low ratings was the lavish illustrations. They seem not planned for helpfulness but rather for color, design, and layout appearance. Businessmen who publish and sell books value these features, but the textbook raters wrote that the illustrations were too abstract, needlessly complicated, and not explained well enough.

A fourth fault is the way student activities are used. In most cases the textbooks failed to connect the results of an activity with the science concepts to be learned. Teachers rated twenty-eight features in all, rating most of them "low" and others "fair."

Good science teachers have long been aware of the mediocre nature of the books supplied to them. Why did lawmakers in the first place include science in their Goals 2000? Because school science already had problems. Research in those earlier days showed that students were progressively turned-off to science, until by graduation only a few wanted to pursue science. American children scored high in international testing at age nine but lower and lower at older ages. In those days science was not taught formally in primary grades, below age nine, so this means that early "homeschooling" and real life served to teach children well up to that age. Then school textbooks, which began at age nine, failed them. In spite of all the Goals 2000 money, there was no improvement.

Homeschoolers now do not have to rely on major public school textbooks. Many smaller publishers have mushroomed. Some of these can be classed as ministry publishers rather than businessman publishers. Most of them are consciously trying to make science more interesting for children. They urge the use of real books as well as real-life activities. They use modern media in many cases, which we must understand are not superior in themselves but only good if the science in them is good. They do add variety though. Some curriculums are built specifically around science demonstrations, somewhat inaccurately called experiments. Several homeschool suppliers provide materials and equipment for science activities. You now have it all. And you can choose quite freely.

Try to determine whether materials you are considering teach important science concepts and not just vocabulary and details that can be easily tested. And try to see whether the activities encourage thinking. Or are they just cookbook-style directions to follow? Sometimes homeschoolers go overboard with the hands-on idea as though children's doing something with their hands is intrinsically better than doing something in their heads. Your children who love to read can learn a lot of science and do a lot of science thinking without activities at all. There is no one magic route to good science learning. Today there are a lot of interesting routes.

The Long Roots of Science

Books sometimes say that the Greeks invented geometry because that was the most ancient geometry that scholars at one time could find. Later, scholars found geometry in Egypt so they began to say that Egyptians invented it, and they guessed that the reason was that Egyptians needed to measure fields along the Nile that flooded each year. Still later, scholars learned that the Sumerians had sophisticated math even before Egypt. All three of those theories are still in books.

These theories about the origins of math are guesswork from people who think in an evolutionary style. They assume that mankind has made progress, progress, progress through the centuries until today when we are smarter than people ever were. This happens in Christian books as well as secular books. Public schooling evidently has programmed practically everybody to think that way.

Bible history shows an opposite picture. God created man with "very good" language and with very good intelligence. God named all the stars. What did He tell Adam? And what did Adam pass on to his sons?

Our hints about the high level of pre-Flood knowledge come from what people knew shortly after the Flood. In the 1900s scholars translated many Sumerian texts and found that Sumerians knew about some planets that we did not "discover" until after the telescope. The Sumerians divided a circle into 360 degrees, and that probably originated from the perfect year of 360 days that existed before the Flood. (See Genesis 7:11 and 8:3–4. Perhaps your children could figure how many months passed and how many days per month that was.) From those numbers, the Sumerians used a number base of sixty, as well as a base of tens. Our dozen is a remnant of the sixties. If we were entirely switched to base ten, we probably would buy cartons of ten eggs instead of twelve eggs. Other ancient peoples used a 366° circle, as the earth now rotates just over 365 times per year when calculated by the sun's rising or just over 366 times when calculated by Venus.

Only recently are some scholars finding out how incredibly sophisticated were ancient measurements with lengths, weights, volumes, and time, all interconnected and tied to the size of the earth. Their calendar worked more accurately than ours today. In the last century scholars found some maps that appear to be copies of copies. They show amazing mathematical knowledge of how to figure exact longitude and to map areas accurately. One map correctly depicts Antarctica, the continent and islands that we can confirm today by satellite imagery.[1] The original map must have been made before Antarctica was covered with ice, and that had to be shortly after Noah's Flood. It took complex cartography and skilled navigating and boat building to make the map. Noah's immediate descendants could well have sailed from pole to pole and mapped their new post-Flood world.

All this early knowledge puzzles scientists who cannot believe that ancient people knew so much. Now they theorize that there was a "lost civilization" somewhere that possessed high-level skills. The Bible answer is that the pre-Flood civilization is the lost civilization the scientists are looking for. This view easily explains how people after the Flood so quickly began using complex math and science again.

Human civilization lost much of its early history and science knowledge at Babel. That catastrophe brought loss of the original language, and people had to reinvent writing systems in their new languages. Some people apparently kept the original Hebrew in which Adam and others wrote the books that passed down to Moses. Later catastrophes destroyed later civilizations in history. And conquerors burned vast libraries. So we have only a spotty history of what early people knew about astronomy and other sciences.

Though very ancient people had a sun-centered system, in Greek times Aristotle taught a geocentric system and most everybody believed him. In the Middle Ages Copernicus formulated the heliocentric system again, but people continued to believe Aristotle. Finally Galileo, Kepler, and Newton verified the sun system and it was accepted—two thousand years after Aristotle. That is the most famous case of scientific close-mindedness.

In areas that challenge the cherished beliefs, science still moves slowly. An "establishment" follows the old beliefs as though they were a religion. The establishment consists of universities, textbook publishers, government, and teachers' unions. That behemoth cannot move easily. It is imperative for science students to not blindly accept views by majority opinion but to think independently. Also, students must learn the Bible well; a true scientific view must ultimately match with the Bible.

Something for Everybody

Students interested in ancient science history will find that field opening up dramatically. Some scientists today are looking with new eyes at the ancient documents. If they tell of violent earth catastrophes, then maybe it was true history, and maybe the movement of comets and planets caused some of the catastrophes. Perhaps the old stories are not just myths after all but have behind them some true history and science. Some of today's homeschoolers may wish to pursue this growing field of study.

Science has something for everybody else, too. We need not limit it to those who think abstractly in math or spatially in engineering. Students talented in those ways can study science specialties according to their interests. Students more interested in people than in things can read biographies of scientists and learn what motivated them, how they worked, and what they contributed to their fellow men.

Students interested in today's cutting-edge science will prefer to learn the latest knowledge of outer space or cells or anything in between. Energy questions are opening up: What about alternatives to oil, and is oil really from fossils? Celestial mechanics is raising questions too. Is gravity the whole of calculating movements of heavenly bodies? Or should electromagnetic forces be added? In biotechnology and nanotechnology things are happening fast.

There is almost no end of exciting fields for science students to study. They should understand the Bible and not get carried into unethical and wasted efforts. Some scientists, for instance, are desperately trying to find life on Mars or elsewhere because then they can believe that somebody "out there" seeded life on Earth and there is no God after all. Others are working just as hard to move mankind forward in his evolution. They tinker with cells and hope to raise life to a higher level. Or they try to combine existing life with smart computers and hope to move evolution forward. Still other scientists study occult phenomena, including extraterrestrial "aliens," not understanding at all the Bible teachings about Satan and his war against God. Your children who understand the Bible will not waste their lives on these useless endeavors. They will study science, instead, with awe for God's great works and with an aim to help people.

Creation Science

The Bible was not lost with ancient libraries. God preserved it through thousands of handwritten copies spread widely. The Bible does not change through the centuries as science does. Many creation scientists today are trying to move the science thinking of society toward the truth of the Bible.

All Christians believe that God created the earth. But some try to fit today's dominant science beliefs together with the Bible in various ways as explained in the worldview chapter. Whatever else you do in science, you should read enough creationist books and discuss these issues enough in your family that you thoroughly clarify your views on evolution versus biblical creation. If you already are clear on this, then make sure your children are too. Only a word or two here and there is not enough. That may be just enough to place them among those who think they are against evolution but cannot explain why. And if they go off to college, they are likely to lose even that shallow faith.

We are fortunate today to have many good books and videos by science writers on these topics.[2] When your children read creationist books, they will also learn evolution, actually better than public school students. The reason is that the books often tell what evolutionists say and then compare it with what creationists say. Public school textbooks tell only the evolution side. This dogmatic, non-critical, one-sided information imprisons students' minds within one view. So they end up understanding evolution theory less well than your children who can see it also from outside the prison.

Here are brief descriptions of some important topics to read about.

Biological evolution. If the world lasts long enough, people will look back and laugh at us for this absurd superstition of biological evolution. We now have enough genetic knowledge to show that biological evolution is impossible. Variations happen, though. People breed both animals and plants to obtain particular characteristics, but they can only go so far. God told each kind to reproduce only its own kind. Some writers call the variations *micro-evolution* and differentiate that from *macro-evolution.* There would be less confusion if we dropped the term micro-evolution and called it variation instead.

There is no shred of proof anywhere for either biological or botanical evolution. Top-tier scientists know this, but don't expect that to filter down into textbooks anytime soon.

Geology and fossils. In geology the evolution books teach layers of earth with names like Cambrian and Jurassic. No place on earth has all the layers. The full chart was formed to show the way geologists thought it would look if one spot did have all the layers. They decided which were lowest and which were next and on upward by what fossils were in each layer. Precambrian has only invertebrates, Cambrian has fish, and so on up to dinosaurs in the Jurassic and man in the Pleistocene, all according to the presumed sequence of the biology evolutionists.

Once the full chart was arranged, biologists used it to date how old particular fossils were. This is called circular reasoning. On one side, biologists date by geologists' theory of layers, and on the other side, geologists date layers by biologists' theory of evolutionary sequence.

In many places the layers are in the "wrong" sequence, so to keep their theories intact, scientists have to figure out how layers were overturned or how they were thrust over other layers. The overthrust idea came from real overthrusts where people can see evidence of disturbance between layers. The same with overturnings. There apparently are real ones. So geologists use overthrusts and overturnings for convenient explanations even in cases where there is no evidence for them.

Fossils in the geology layers also do not help the evolution theories. If biological evolution happened, scientists should find examples of gradual changes from one species to another. They find, instead, distinct differences. Wings are fully formed. Eyes and other organs likewise. They never find eyes halfway developed, on their way to becoming eyes. Evolutionists need millions of transitional links, yet our media occasionally hypes somebody's claim to have found *a single* missing link.

The fossils and geological layers present numerous problems for evolutionists. Bible believers answer most of the problems with their Flood theory that massive upheavals during and immediately after Noah's Flood would form layers in various sequences. Moreover, those upheavals would bury creatures suddenly, thus causing fossilization. Students who read the Flood geology books repeatedly see what evolution says about an evidence and what Flood geology says about the same evidence. So they do not miss out on public school science; they actually learn more.

Physics. The all-encompassing science of physics tries to figure out the fundamental forces of the universe. Two major ideas are matter and energy, and since the atomic age we see that matter *is* energy. So energy is everything, and physics has brought us two laws of energy that are more substantiated than any other laws of science.

1. Law of *conservation* says that the total amount of energy and matter remains the same; it may change form but never disappears,

2. Law of *entropy* says that energy is never used fully, one hundred percent; some always deteriorates into unusable form. Thus the world is running down, not evolving upward.

Energy and matter combine in Einstein's special theory of relativity that says the energy from an object equals its mass times the speed of light squared: $E = mc^2$. Did you memorize that in high school? That theory is the base of physics, and in it Einstein used the current science view of the speed of light. That raises this question: If a star is many light years away, then how do we see it if it was created only six thousand years ago? That is probably the greatest problem now for young earthers to work on.

Many ancient peoples followed Aristotle's belief that the speed of light was instantaneous, that it took no time at all to reach us. Even famous astronomers like Johannes Kepler in the 1600s believed this. So the current belief is not long lived. Science always changes. The Bible does not.

Evolutionists believe either that the universe has no beginning or that it began—somehow—with a big bang billions of years ago. Neither of these beliefs follow their two physics laws mentioned above. A big bang could not occur while the amount of energy remained constant, and the billions of years could not occur while deterioration operated all that time. The Earth would long ago have deteriorated to uninhabitability. Bible beliefs fit well with the two laws. There was a beginning. God created and set everything in working order. Then sin brought a curse upon the world, and this was the start of the second law. Someday God will remove the curse and set up a new Heaven and new Earth.

National Science Education Standards

The National Science Education Standards for curriculum specifically state that there is no arbitrary sequence of content. When you see a listing of what to learn in fourth grade, what to learn in fifth and so on, that list is made for graded schools so the fifth grade teacher will not repeat what the fourth grade teacher taught. As a homeschooler, you are free from that arbitrariness.

Nobody can "cover" science. The best you can do is try to acquaint your children with parts of the four categories of science content listed in the national standards:

1. Physical science
2. Life science
3. Earth and space science
4. Science and technology

Touching on all four during the journey to grade twelve will give students the ability to read more intelligently about current issues and controversies. It provides this "general education" in science that all citizens need. It will provide a base for specializing and advancing in a particular field if a student desires to do so. And it provides the breadth that even science specialists need. Some scientists believe they lose a lot by having too narrow a focus.

No person or curriculum can specify exactly what your child *should* learn. The standards explain that the traditional way was to limit inquiry and investigations in order to try to cover large amounts of content. They recommend the opposite—spend more time on investigations even if it means uneven attention to content areas. So if you spend more time on space and less time on insects, that is fine as long as children are learning to ask questions and seek answers. Provide plenty of reading for the "readers" in your family and videos for everybody. Try science kits for those who will use them in particular topics. And watch for opportunities to use nature or machines or anything real.

Besides the four content categories listed above, the national standards list four ideas about science. Items 5 to 8 describe these briefly.

5. *Science as inquiry.* Students at elementary levels and at high school levels can learn to ask questions if they have interesting science books to read. They can seek answers, not necessarily with test tubes and such, but often with books or with the world around them.

6. *History and nature of science.* For the history of science, biographies work well. For the nature of science, the biblical view is that there is order in the universe, thus we can find order and laws by studying the earth and the universe. Evolutionists look for laws, too, and do not notice the inconsistency with their basic beliefs. The evolutionary basic view is that everything is haphazard and random, with no intelligent designer behind it all.

7. *Science in personal and social perspective.* Personal perspectives of science can include study of nutrition and natural supplements, and any medical and disease topics. Use this opportunity to begin with a family need and learn a lot about it. Social perspectives is the area where schools teach current political views on population and environment. These have grown controversial with some views being called "junk science," in which people distort science findings in order to promote their particular political agenda. For instance, some people hold an unbiblical view that our population interferes with animal "rights" and with the earth itself. You can explore any of these issues, remembering to connect with your biblical views.

8. *Unifying concepts and processes in science.* The major concept taught in schools and secular books, particularly in biology, is evolution. It permeates science books and materials, beginning with

little children's dinosaur books. The major Bible *concept* is that God designed and created. A major *process* is finding order and organization, and evidences for the concepts. Creationists and evolutionists both try to work this way. A process that young children can begin learning is measurement. All science researches involve measuring something in some way.

These eight listings in the national standards contain so much that all children can find plenty to read about and to do. They cannot "cover" everything, but they can continue growing in interest and knowledge of science.

Through the Grades

Primary. In terms of standard grade levels, primary means up through third grade. Homeschoolers are good at individualizing, and they are not rigid about that boundary, flexing it forward or backward as needed for any particular child.

The main job of primary children is to acquire the skills of reading and writing (and numbers). They can use any content for those language skills, science sometimes included. They will learn some science naturally as you visit the zoo, tend your garden, teach health habits, and experience other life activities. Your children may play with toy animals, magnets, balloons. They mix colors, spin tops, and so on. All such activities are natural science learning for young children, even though they look like play.

Primaries can enjoy children's books on science topics. You read or the child reads, just as you do with storybooks. There is an abundance of science books on a primary level so, as the national standards specify, they can read topics in any order.

Elementary and middle school. Since you are not bound to cover particular topics in particular grades, continue acquainting your children with the four broad categories of science knowledge listed in the national standards. Some books today make chemistry and other topics highly appealing to children. They tell interesting stories of scientists and their discoveries, teaching a lot of information this way rather than with technical and mathematical approaches.

Some books focus on activities. Students who find reading difficult, for whatever reason, like this hands-on approach. These are often the students who gravitate to math and science subjects and end up as engineers. During the grades and on through high school, try to let your "non-readers" learn more from videos and science kits and activities. You might locate opportunity for these students to apprentice or spend time with a friend who works in a science field. Try, also, to keep their reading and writing progressing as much as you can.

Some "readers" may not enjoy what we call hands-on science activities. Other students may seem more balanced between learning from reading and learning from activities. So avoid labeling children as either hands-on or reader types. Each child has an individual mix of those interests and abilities. You can use most homeschool science materials with most children, learning to adapt them as you go along, especially for children who lean heavily toward the activity or toward the read-only modes of learning. Children need the kinds of learning they like best, but they need some of the others, too.

Besides books for learning, use local field trips and museum visits. You can use science kits on particular topics that your children become interested in. Some homeschool groups plan co-ops in science for families particularly afraid of science; but with all the good materials available now, co-ops are less important. Science clubs and math clubs are growing in popularity. Written reports are not necessary after every book or museum trip. Sometimes skip these or let children explain orally what they learned. Remember to value the thinking *processes* of inquiry and investigation that students experience more than the *products*—their reports. If they enter science fairs or other contests then, of course, the reports and displays are important.

High school. Homeschoolers have opened up high school learning to any and every kind of system that works for them, and that has greatly improved education in these teen years. Many college science professors say they prefer homeschoolers to public school students. Remember the failure of Goals 2000 science? That effort required American high school students to take more science courses, yet American students scored almost at the bottom among first-world nations in science. Homeschoolers pursuing science arrive at college with a refreshing attitude of earnestly wanting to learn. They bring knowledge too, some of them even having earned advanced placement by passing AP tests during high school. Or they save money in college by passing some courses with the college level examination program (CLEP) tests.

Teens often prefer "courses." They like the feeling of closure when they complete a course. So you and your teen could plan what to do for a course. Try to break out from the traditional school-type textbook. Innovative courses from homeschool publishers may look good to you. On Internet you can pursue open-ended learning in practically any topic. You also can find courses there. You can use videos, science kits, and CDs, according to your budget and the student's interest. And don't forget real books. They enrich especially a textbook course. For transcripts, you can record the reading and activities after the fact. That is easier than planning everything in detail ahead of time. Transcript helps are easy to find on the Internet.

Do your teens want to pursue science as a major, or are their interests elsewhere? For all students, help them learn some science for their general education. For college-bound students, give attention to the usual college entrance requirements, but feel free to meet these in creative ways, rather than locking into the school textbook system. Structured curriculums cost more than regular trade books. A librarian explained to a homeschool mother, "We don't carry science textbooks because we can get the same information for less money in other books." The real books not only save money—lots of it in the case of science—but they also are the way to handle homeschool with multi-aged students. All can study stars or oceans at the same time.

Some students may reach high school without the background they need for tackling science courses. One mother lamented that the vocabulary in a biology text was overwhelming. Did her child really need to understand that? If your student reaches such a place, one technique is to find children's books on the topics, and read and talk about them. Children's writers work hard to be accurate and to explain complex ideas in simple ways. Their books are a boon to non-science parents as well as to students. Reading such books can help provide the missing background and build the needed vocabulary. Then you could return to the biology book and try the textbook skills given in the study skills chapter.

Some students are advanced and highly motivated in science studies. They can take courses at a community college or take online college courses while they are still high school age. If you take too many college courses while in high school, you may not qualify for a freshman scholarship. Check with the college counselor about this.

Science students need plenty of math, and here you need planned curriculum more than in other subjects. There is no point in using the kind planned for classrooms where you have to buy a teacher book, student textbook, student workbook, tests, answer keys, and maybe associated videos or other helps. The cost of all that classroom stuff is way up there. Also, there is no point in looking for color and glitz (which cost more), although practically all publishers these days think that is necessary to sell books. The science-minded students usually can learn from any ol' book. One boy said, "Don't worry, Mom. Just get an algebra book and I'll learn algebra."

With all the helpful materials available today, you need not fear science. Just dive in and enjoy it along with your students.

Lists

For high school students the transcript and your notes in preparation for that provide a record of science learning. For younger children try keeping lists of learning activities as they do them. Here are some suggested categories for the lists:

- Books by creation scientists
- Videos and audios by creation scientists
- Other science books
- Other videos and audios
- Projects (include the calendar problem from Genesis 7:11 and 8:3–4)
- Units
- Field trips

Form a list of topics that you or the children wish to learn more about when you can manage the time. (The suggestions and lists that appear throughout this book can serve as brief reminders of what you have read in the preceding section. Or, depending on your family situation, you may use some of the ideas for teaching your children.)

4 Worldviews to Match the Bible

In Christian homeschooling, worldview teaching means passing on to children biblical views of important matters in life and society. Some parents may think that children will "catch" their views, so they do not specifically teach them. But no, children do not catch much of this. Somebody has to explain why abortion is wrong or how communism is not biblical. Such topics are easier to handle in homeschooling families than in families where children spend a great deal of time learning their values from non-Christian peers.

Teaching these views requires awareness on your part so you can take advantage of opportune moments when they come along. This chapter suggests some major worldview topics and some ideas for correlating them with the Bible and Christianity.

Bible Only

A powerful Bible-only approach to worldviews appeared in a magazine interview with Dr. John MacArthur.[1] He said, "Nobody ever taught me 'Biblical Worldview, Christian Worldview.' I never had that growing up. My parents just taught me the Bible, and I saw the world through the Bible."

Your children, he says, will encounter worldly trends and they will need to buck the tide. The way to protect them is by simply teaching the Word of God. A book to help is *Think Biblically: Recovering a Christian Worldview.*[2] MacArthur was general editor of this book that he and colleagues wrote because they found no clear book on this topic. He says it really is a theology book. "All it is, is God on this topic or that topic or the other topic." It defines "certain key themes that everybody is aware of: origins, morality, the role of women, the role of men, the arts, science—those kinds of things. And giving God's Word on those is really just another way to frame a theology." This is probably the clearest and most straightforward definition of Christian worldview to be found anywhere; just see what the Bible says about each topic. This book could well be part of your homeschool reading.

As president of The Master's College, MacArthur sees many homeschoolers arrive and sees them generally perform as their best students. The college aims to protect and preserve what you have worked to instill in your children. They do not undermine the Christian worldview as most colleges do today, even Christian colleges. A girl at a Christian college heard nonbiblical views in biology class, psychology class, and others. She said to a professor, "I thought in a Christian school we would learn Bible views." The professor answered, "We are trying to open your minds." The majority of Christian colleges today fall into that category, so it is up to parents more than ever to teach Bible worldviews and to provide guidance about which college to attend.

Evolution and Young Earth

From ancient times the anti-God view of evolution opposed the God-is-Creator view. Sometimes it had other names, like "Great Chain of Being," but this false belief has a long history and it underlies today's false worldviews such as humanism and communism. It leads to most of society's ills; if man descended from ape-like creatures, then he has no reason to live as though he will answer to his Creator.

News stories about occasional school district battles usually misreport the issues. They use propaganda terms like *equal time* and *teaching religion,* when those are not at all what people are asking for. To see these issues clearly, your family needs to be informed about the major points of the evolution controversy. This section provides an overview of what those points are.

The evolution controversy is closely tied to the old-earth versus young-earth controversy. If you believe in a young earth, you believe it is about six thousand years old according to a literal reading of the Bible. If you believe in an old earth, you believe it is billions of years old, according to scientists. Few Christians say they believe in evolution, but many say they believe in an old earth.

But evolution and old earth go together. Evolutionists need all those years in their theory because they cannot see how living creatures could evolve in a short time. They do not see how life could form in billions of years, either, but they are trying to think it could. There is no Bible reason whatever for Christians to believe in an old earth. The reason some do is that they are going along with the scientists. They have a faith that science must be right, so they have to somehow make the Bible fit today's science.

One idea for fitting the Bible to old-earth science is called the age-day theory. In this, people say each creation day in Genesis 1 is a long age. That would mean plants created on day three must wait a long age for day four before the sun shines on them. Another argument against age days is the way Genesis 1 uses the word *day*. They are all numbered: day one, day two, and so on. Every other place in the Bible where a number accompanies the word day it refers to a normal calendar day, not an indefinite period. So it stretches logic to make exception only in Genesis 1. The verses also define the boundaries of each day: the evening and the morning were the first day. Still another Bible argument is the words God wrote in stone with His finger. The words command His people to keep the Sabbath day holy because God rested that seventh day after six days of creating. It is nonsense to say the Sabbath is like a long age when God rested.

Another idea for fitting the Bible to old-earth is the gap theory. In this theory people propose a gap of time after Genesis 1:1. God created the heaven and the earth, they say, and it existed for the billions of years that the evolutionists want. Animals lived and died, many of them catastrophically so they became fossils. After all that gap of time, God took a week to renew or recreate everything. Adam and the human race began. A variation of this theory is that long gaps occurred between each creation day, and God periodically stepped in and created something. The Bible problem with age-long gaps is that death began with Adam's sin, so there could not be eons filled with death and destruction before Adam. When God looked at everything on the sixth day, He pronounced it "good," not full of violence and death. So the gap theory does not satisfy Bible theology of sin and salvation. Neither does it satisfy evolutionary scientists. Their whole point in working out such a theory is to find a way to explain things without God.

The age-day theory and the gap theory stretch and contort the Bible account all out of sense. A different kind of theory is the poetry theory. People say that Genesis 1 is not narrative history, but poetry. By this they usually imply that its meaning is fuzzy and we cannot really know it; poetry is just a bunch of fancy words that give us a general feeling about its topic. A recent linguistic study refutes that theory. Dr. Steven W. Boyd of The Master's College compared narrative and poetry sections of the Bible and found a distinct difference in the forms of verbs used. Then he applied this test to Genesis 1 and found that the verbs used identify it as narrative, with a probability of almost one hundred percent, extremely high as statistical probabilities run. Besides this scientific study of narration versus poetry, a more casual reader can easily see that it does not contain metaphoric imagery, or parallel couplet forms, or any other hint of being a poem.[3]

Besides Bible reasons to believe in a young earth, numerous physical processes that scientists study also show a young age. For instance, the earth's magnetic field is decaying, and this decay could not have continued for even one million years. The magnetic field would be completely gone. A few other such clocks for measuring earth's age are: river deltas; lead, iron, and other chemicals carried into the oceans by rivers; decay of short-period and long-period comets; influx of radiocarbon to earth; and influx of meteoritic dust from space.

There are plenty of science reasons for believing in a young earth and even more science reasons for being anti-evolution. Actually, there is not one evidence anywhere for evolution. The old-earth faith is a prop to try to bolster up evolution. If we had eons of time, the theory says, then possibly somewhere somehow evolution could have happened. And someday someone might discover how.

Recent science discoveries, though, are bad news for the evolutionists. They are showing that evolution is impossible. What scientists have learned about genetics and the DNA code show that one kind of creature cannot change into another kind. The DNA code will allow for variation such as all the varieties of dogs that we have. But dogs cannot change into horses, either suddenly or gradually over billions of years. Many biologists now admit in their writings that biological evolution is impossible. Yet scientists in other fields, as well as historians, teachers, and all kinds of people think that biologists have proved evolution.

Top-tier scientists are discussing and writing about these problems, but the teachers' union and other political powers so far have managed to keep out all mention of evolution's problems. They do not allow what should be the scientific kind of study, which would examine both the claims and the problems of evolution and old-earth theory. They want it taught as fact, not theory.

Homeschoolers are free from artificial political restrictions. You can use wonderful materials supplied by creationist organizations,[4] and open up your children's minds to both sides of the issues. Children will be better thinkers by seeing the issues from inside and out, and then they can better explain and defend their own worldview. (More on evolution is in the science chapter.)

While Christians may need to read up on creationist views, evolutionists, too, are often quite ignorant about evolution. A talk-show host pounced on a caller, put her down as a religious idiot, and said, "We know from carbon dating that the earth is billions of years old." With that he exposed his shallow knowledge of chemical dating. The radiocarbon method cannot measure billions of years. It measures only a few thousand years. A high school science teacher was asked, "Do your classes ever discuss the evolution controversy?" He responded sharply, "They could argue the theory of gravity if they want to." That was his way of saying it was a foolish question; who in his right mind would argue something as sure as gravity or as evolution. With that he revealed his non-knowledge of top-tier evolutionists who do in fact raise numerous questions about evolution theory.

If talk-show hosts would read even one or two books written by creation scientists, they could carry on better conversations. If teachers would read even one book by a sharp-thinking evolution-ist, they could have more exciting classes. Likewise, your family can read at least one or two books by creation scientists so your children can give reasons for their worldview. All views are not equal in value. That is the whole point of schooling. Why study if one view is as good as another?

Teaching Suggestion

List at least two books on evolution problems or age of the earth that your children read.[4]

_____

_____

Religions

We use the term "New Age" to refer to many of today's religions. There is nothing new in New Age. It encompasses the ancient pagan beliefs and practices of the Greeks, Egyptians, and Celts, and those of today's Hindus, Buddhists, Taoists, and Native American religions. One writer said that New Age is far too exten-sive to cover it adequately in less than a few thousand pages. To simplify the matter we can just lump together all the practices like witchcraft, channeling the spirits, transcendental meditation, astrology, fortune-telling, and so on. The old satanic lies are now called New.

There are two classes of New Agers. One class can be called the social New Agers. They go along because it seems the trendy thing to do. They talk about the coming Aquarian age, about reincarnation, and other current beliefs. They may practice yoga, meditation, solstice dances, and other popular activities.

The other class, serious New Agers, studies and works "The Plan" of world unity, an immensely complex idea where matter and spirit meld into one. They believe we all evolve into the collective oneness.

A third class of people, though not religious minded, get pulled into helping the New Agers without knowing that they are helping. Here is where New Age touches our lives. We see it daily in politics and world events. One strategy New Agers use to pull in the unwary is the environmental movement. This unites people in preparing the "living" planet Gaia—Mother Earth—for the coming of their Christ figure. It is biblical to care for the earth, of course, but it is not biblical to go to the extremes of some activists, such as placing animal "rights" above or equal to human rights. Only humans are made in the image of God, not animals. But in the New Age universalist, oneness view, all is sacred. God is in all; all is God—people and animals alike. And the earth itself.

New Age movements often drop the word *Age* and speak of the new spirituality instead. That term can fit into churches, they think. They form "peace" organizations, and that can fit into our politics. They are clever at using words we like, even the name *Jesus*, but giving different meanings to them.

Not too long ago we could talk safely about mystical eastern religions. They were "over there," and we were comfortably over here in our western civilization. The West owes its science and clear thinking patterns to Christianity, but we are now departing from Christianity. That allows eastern mysticism to invade. This attracts some by its occultism and gains fellow travelers by unity thinking and unity movements. These movements want us to work together on saving the earth or merging the nations into one.

God did not tell people to unify their nations. After the Flood He commanded that people spread throughout the earth. They disobeyed and formed the first united nations at Babel, so God intervened and forced them to disperse. Genesis 10 names seventy nations with separate lands and languages that began at that time.

Unity thinking also infects the church. The true Church, capital C, is already unified in Christ. Jesus prayed that His people would be one, and God made them one in His Spirit. People need not answer Jesus' prayer. God is the one who answers prayers. The fast-spreading unity movement in churches wants us to ignore our core beliefs because they divide. In effect, believe nothing very strongly. That unites. Are the unity movements preparing a world church and a world government to be ready for the antichrist?

The most effective homeschool approach to help children follow the Bible path is to teach the Bible often and thoroughly. Then without studying thousands of pages of New Age error, or error of other religions, children can learn to recognize error because it does not match the Bible.

Islam. Islam surrounds us these days, and schoolbooks and major media so misrepresent it that it pays to do a little direct teaching on it. Islam does not lump in with New Age religions, but we can lump it with all false religions. Some of the false teachings in the Koran are listed below. Words in quotations are directly from the Koran.

1. Jesus is not the Son of God, "only a messenger of Allah." Those who say He is a "partner" with God will enter the

"Gates of hell," be dragged through boiling water and thrust into the fire. It is "certain they did not crucify Jesus." "Allah took him up unto Himself." At the last moment they substituted Judas for Jesus.

2. God cannot have a son. Those who think He does are disbelievers and idolaters.

3. Muslims are commanded to wage war on all disbelievers. "Warfare [Jihad] is ordained for you." "Slay the idolaters wherever you find them." The angel will "smite the necks and smite of them each finger" because they opposed Allah and his messenger Mohammed. "Allah is severe in punishment."

4. Bible stories are scrambled. The first sanctuary appointed for mankind was Mecca, "the place where Abraham stood up to pray." The angels fell prostrate before Adam, all except Satan. The brothers begged to take Joseph with them into the fields instead of the father sending him to find the brothers.

5. There is marriage in heaven. The faithful can recline on couches in delightful gardens and wed "fair ones with wide, lovely eyes." Servants will bring as much fruit and meat as they desire.

Several good adult-level books now inform about the history and beliefs of Islam. They say things that political leaders are not able to say and that major media avoid.[5] Good books for children are more rare, but one good book by a missionary organization is *Learning about Islam*[6] for children eight and up. Children using this will assemble a booklet each on Christianity and Islam to compare the two. What is the name of the founder, the holy book, and the God of each? How is one saved in each? The book tells true stories from Muslim lands and from America. It teaches clearly about terrorism, but avoids graphic depictions of violence and ugliness. For instance: in prison "they treated him badly." It even uses humor in this unhumorous subject. In a skit an American boy talks with a Muslim friend who spends hours a day reading and memorizing the Koran. Brian witnesses to him about the Bible but runs into a bit of trouble.

> **Khalid:** How many hours a day do you study your Bible?
> **Brian:** Hours? A day? Uh . . .

It will be difficult for anyone to outdo this children's introduction to Islam.

Humanism. Modern humanists clearly state that they are nontheists; they begin with humans and not God, with nature and not God. All Bible believers would instantly recognize errors such as that salvation and heaven are illusions. Perhaps less clear are the ways they use words like dogmatic, proselytize, intolerant, and irrational. Christians are dogmatic to believe the Bible is true, but humanists are not dogmatic to believe their way is right and our way is wrong. Christians are proselytizing to display Christian symbols. They are intolerant if their view differs on homosexuality or other matters.

Humanism is anti-biblical through and through. It permeates today's schools, media, and political debates. Almost daily you can read or hear something that provides an opportunity to point out to your children how it differs from the Bible. This may be difficult at first if you have not practiced it yet. Humanists are skilled at communication. They make their views sound so good that Christians can be lured into agreeing. Watch for the tricky use of words like *dogmatic* or *intolerance.* Watch for political or societal issues that your children can understand well enough to compare with the Bible. After the news or other opportune occasions, point out something unbiblical and have a brief conversation about it. When your children begin spotting and pointing out to you the unbiblical thinking, give them an *A*. Or give yourself an *A* for successful teaching.

The roots of humanism go back at least to the beginning of anti-God religion—to the people who believed the serpent's promise that they could become wise like God. That religion spread everywhere. The Greeks embraced it in their thinking. Plato, Socrates, and other famous philosophers thought they could find truth by their own reasoning. They asked important questions like what is mind, what is soul, and is there life after death. What is the origin of man? What is evil? Greek philosophers tried to solve those big questions by human reason alone. This sharpening of the human intellect was a major aim of Greek education, and modern humanism descends from those Greek roots.

On its way to us from ancient Greece, humanism passed through the Italian Renaissance. The Italians coined the name humanism. Latin *umanisa* was equivalent to "classicist" or "classical scholar." History textbooks present this humanism of the Renaissance as a major turning point in western civilization, and this thinking still lives today.

To bring this humanism into Christian education is to try to merge paganism with Christianity. Humanist thinking opposes biblical thinking and unless we can push it back, our children's generation will be promoting it even more stridently than ours.

Checklist

List religious topics that you wish to talk about so your children will understand better.

New Age   _____

Islam   _____

Humanism   _____

_____

_____

Government and Politics

A good strategy for helping your children become aware of various forms of government is the same as with all worldviews: begin with what children meet in their lives. In their reading they will probably meet mostly with kings and emperors. The Bible teaches that kings will not work well until Jesus becomes King. He is perfectly righteous, so He will be the perfect King. Men are sinful, some worse than others, so human kings are sinful. Kings are not elected; they serve for life. Sometimes we call them dictators or emperors. Today we may even call them presidents, but if they are really dictators they are always "reelected" by fraudulent means. When particular rulers are in the news, you can help children understand something about what kind of rulers they are.

The people of Israel asked the prophet Samuel to give them a king. Samuel prayed and God told him what a king would be like for the people. First, he would take their sons to serve him and to be in the military, whereas in the time of the judges the military was voluntary, called up only at times when needed. A king also would take the daughters to serve him. He would require taxes of their crops and animals, and he would confiscate fields and give them to his servants (1 Samuel 8:4–18). A story of confiscating a field is told in 1 Kings 21:1–16. Another story of the burden of kings is in 1 Kings 12:1–19.

Solomon's son Rehoboam consulted with the old men who had worked with Solomon, and they said the people would love him if he would serve them and be good to them. Then he consulted with the young men his own age, and they told him to make the people's burden even heavier than Solomon had. Rehoboam listened to the young men. He sent a tax collector to the tribes of Israel and the people stoned him. That part of the kingdom split away and took a different king. American colonists did the same thing. When the king's burdens became too heavy they did not exactly stone the tax collectors but they threw their tea overboard at Boston, and they split away from England.

The founders of America knew from Isaiah 33:22 that government requires three functions: *For the LORD is our judge, the LORD is our lawgiver, the LORD is our king. . . .* In Christ's kingdom Jesus will be judge and lawgiver and king, but in earthly kingdoms people are sinful, and governments become corrupt if too much power is placed under one person. So the founders formed three branches of government and divided the powers into judicial, legislative, and executive. Each branch could watch the others and try to keep them from being like Rehoboam.

Governments tend to continually take more power to themselves. In communism, the leaders have all power over everything. In freer nations people fear the word communism, so clever leaders use other words instead. One word is socialism. Another is progressivism. That sounds good until you investigate what they want to progress toward. Many movements by other names are ways the communists hide their true colors.

Current labels in American politics that children can begin to understand are conservatives and liberals. Conservatives stand for smaller government, smaller taxes, and people running their own lives without too much government interference. Liberals stand for big government running all kinds of programs for people, which naturally require big taxes too. Republicans are supposed to be more conservative, but in practice, many officials from both parties vote for government programs that pass out taxpayer money because that will earn them votes from the people who receive the largess. The meanings of labels and political parties change over time in history.

Use current events as well as your history and civics studies to help children gradually understand the complex matters of government, and always try to compare with Bible principles.

Checklist

Here is a list of topics you may wish to talk about or read with your children:

What kings will do (1 Samuel 8:4–18)	_____
What King Ahab did (1 Kings 21:1–16)	_____
What King Rehoboam did (1 Kings 12:1–19)	_____
America's three branches of government	_____
Communism	_____
Conservative	_____
Liberal	_____

Family and Society

The very first institution that God ordained was the family. Before church, before government, before school, came family. Families build society. Christian families living righteously build a strong society. Unbiblical family patterns break down society.

God created man in His own image, and He told Noah that there should be a death sentence for murder: *Whoso sheddeth man's blood, by man shall his blood be shed: for in the image of God made he man* (Genesis 9:6). Having a death sentence for murder clearly is biblical. Homosexuality clearly is unbiblical—as well as abortion and adultery. Many societal problems stem from people not knowing or following the Bible's plain and simple teachings. Sadly, many Christian teens do not know these teachings either. Parents at a conference took a survey of their children to determine their opinions on several worldview topics, and their answers shocked the parents, who were all homeschool leaders gathered at the conference. They had to realize that their children did not pick up their beliefs, and they had better specifically teach them in the future. Some large polls show that up to eighty-five percent of church-going students leave their faith when they go to college. Apparently, churches and families need to strengthen their Bible teaching.

Teaching important Bible truths is a major task of Christian homeschoolers. Be sure your children know the teachings from Adam's and Noah's times. Be sure they know the Ten Commandments, even memorize them. Add Jesus' Sermon on the Mount. He goes further than teaching that acts of murder and adultery are wrong. He says do not even think in those directions—don't hate, don't lust. Move on in the Bible to Paul's teaching about not being unequally yoked with unbelievers. Children should learn this while they are young and learn the danger of becoming emotionally involved with a non-Christian. They must learn it before they become involved.

To help your children know what you believe, use bits of conversation concerning a news story or an experience of a friend or acquaintance and, of course, use conversation about the Bible. This is "immersion" teaching; children are immersed in a climate of biblical worldviews. A major reason that families choose to homeschool is to avoid immersing their children in the climate of peers with unbiblical views, and many parents develop the habit of teaching their important views. Teachings about family are especially important because we cannot assume or hope that the church will do it adequately. At times you may not know yet what your opinion is on something, but you can be firm on your opinion that the Bible is the best and true guide for living.

Since your children grow up without constant influence of a peer group their own age, at times when they are in such a group they may feel out of place. They cannot join the conversation about movie stars, music icons, and TV programs. It often helps to state simply that other people may do or think that, but we do this. It is OK to be different. In fact, it is necessary when biblical standards are involved. While society moves away from the Bible and its principles, your home can be an oasis of right living and thinking.

Checklist

List important family and society topics that you have talked about or wish to talk about with your children.

Death sentence   ____

Homosexuality   ____

Abortion   ____

Drugs   ____

_____   ____

_____   ____

5   Thinking Skills

A mother and four children age five and under were watching a television program called "Barney." The mother asked, "Have you guys ever noticed that when Baby Bop turns around you can see the zipper in her costume?" The children were shocked at first to realize it was a costume, but it opened to them a new manner of thinking during their weekly television sessions. One week the mother walked in and heard the four-year-old say, "Well, I think they just turn off the camera, rearrange the studio, and then turn the camera back on" (to get outside quickly). The five-year-old responded, "Maybe you're right. You can tell that it's just a painting in the background, and the trees don't look real."

Those children never studied a course on observing the data, making a hypothesis, and drawing conclusions. They already have thinking minds. God made them that way. And as this mother operates, they will continue to use their thinking minds in everyday life. Later on, school subjects become a part of everyday life and children should think in those too. Math thinking in math, science thinking in science, people thinking in history and literature, and so on. This system works better than learning to think in a separate thinking class and then expecting to transfer the skills to other classes. Transfer is limited.

Children even younger than five already demonstrate their God-given thinking abilities. Toddler Jay was sitting on the edge of the wash basin being bathed by his mother. He showed terror as water disappeared down the drain. His mother immediately tightened her arm around him so he could feel secure from going down the drain himself. Then she took objects one at a time and asked if they could go down. No, the ball couldn't go down. The bar of soap couldn't. The duck couldn't. Too big. When Jay relaxed his tension, the mother asked, "Could Jay go down?" A brief hesitation, then "No."

Jay needed only to observe the concrete objects. His inbuilt thinking skills took over from there, just as observing the zipper triggered a long train of thinking in the television watchers.

Another example. Three-year-old Aaron was entering his bedroom when the light from the room behind caused his shadow to shoot up the wall in front of him to monster proportions. He screamed, and his mother picked him up and turned away from the monster. Fortunately the mother had seen that incident and knew what caused Aaron's fear of the bedroom. For the next several days she and Aaron walked in the sunlight and observed their shadows—Mother's bigger, Aaron's shorter. They played the game of stepping on each other's shadow. In the house they made shadows of objects in the lamplight. Then came the day they decided to make Aaron's shadow on the wall. "Let's turn on the light in this room. Now let's go to the bedroom door." The monster appeared and Aaron tensed in a brief burst of fear but immediately relaxed as he understood.

The child had no abstract teaching on cause and effect thinking, let alone the physics of light or geometry of sizes. All he needed was experience on what we call the concrete level—experience with reality. With both Jay and Aaron, the mother happened to be able to take part. Even without that guidance, child thinking continues all the time, while climbing rocks, wading in water, handling objects, playing independently in the yard. The English grandparents in one family wanted to landscape the somewhat wild backyard into an elegant no-touch, just-look English style. But the mother said no. She instinctively knew that the children's minds and imaginations had more to work with the way it was. All young children naturally learn from concrete experiences. We just need to let it happen.

Family Thinking Activities

Children of all ages can practice thinking in everyday family life. Should the family buy something on time or save up and pay cash? They have to consider data on interest payments and how urgently the family needs the item and what alternative there might be to buying one. Let the children help solve big problems and little problems that occur in daily life. A book on finances for Christian families may suggest some ideas for your family to discuss.[1]

Newspaper cartoons are wonderful for family conversation. The humor requires a high level of thinking. Jokes and cartoons are funny only to people who understand what the humorist is saying. Political cartoons require some knowledge of current political happenings, and children can learn a bit of that just through talking about a cartoon. Who or what is this person? Why is he doing this? Which characters stand for real persons? If one is not named, what exaggerated features give you a clue? Compare with a photo if possible. One might be in yesterday's newspaper account of the situation being cartooned. Cartoons are full of analogies and other thinking skills, plus they are a fun way to keep up a little with current events. This family activity is so valuable that if you do not receive a paper yourself it is worth scrounging up some from work or a neighbor or somewhere.

Graphs in publications are another food for thinking. Children can try to understand all that the graph is saying. Take time to see what the numbers on the sides and bottom stand for. Why do the lines or the bars rise and fall? Could you make the line rise less steeply or more steeply by arranging the size of the units differently? Learning graphs in arithmetic class is for the purpose of using graphs. Help your children transfer arithmetic learning to daily life where all of us meet graphs even if our occupation does not use them. Besides graphs, also study details on other kinds of charts.

Games are great for thinking. Ancient games like chess and checkers have survived for the very reason that they engage the mind so fully. To play games you must analyze and strategize. Think ahead. What will happen if you do this or the other? Compare your choices. What might the opponent do? And so on. Even simple games for very young children require thinking skills. We may assume they are all chance and no strategy. But there is a sequence of moves and events to learn, and some hoping that the spinner will land at a good point, and usually some counting—counting that matters more than the practice in arithmetic class.

There was a time in homeschooling when the writings warned you about games. You could play them if they were "educational." *Authors* was OK because children learned the book and author facts. More author-like games appeared with other facts. The strategy and thinking in all games were ignored. Only if you learned some facts were they viewed as educational.

Then schools sponsored chess clubs because of what they did for thinking and for attention spans of some children who had difficulty focusing. This helped homeschoolers to accept chess too. Chess and other games could do much for your children's thinking habits. We are overrun with computer games today, but do not forget the old-fashioned table games. They provide family fellowship and bonding along with promoting thinking skills.

Junk mail and ads provide good material for thinking. These commonly use testimonials from individuals. This and that person were healed remarkably or made more money. Help children recognize this technique. To make a good decision they need information on how and why the product works, not just testimonials from individuals they do not know. Another technique is image. Good-looking people or famous people are shown with the product. Before-and-after pictures can be faked, or at least exaggerated. Is the girl smiling in the second picture but not in the first?

Some ads provide arithmetic thinking. Does one tell only the monthly payment and avoid telling the total cost? Does one promise to "save" money on your monthly payments, but when you think through the procedure you find that it costs extra money in interest over longer periods of time? Are statistics misused? A radio ad urges you to buy a phonics kit because "research shows that three out of four children need extra help in learning to read." What's wrong with this picture? (Three-fourths of children cannot be the small group at the low end that needs *extra* help.)

If your family has to sit through television commercials, try using the time to analyze the ad techniques. A thinking family always has plenty to talk about.

Propaganda

Propaganda is all around us, not only in ads but in much of the news and issues of the day. Propaganda disseminates mostly derogatory information. It is biased and misleading and promotes a particular point of view. This meaning came into use only about a century ago. Before that Christians used the word to refer to propagating the faith.

Nowadays propaganda is a "dirty word," and all kinds of groups seeking power or other results in society use it. An example from the 1920s was a nature organization in California successfully obtaining a ban on development of coal mining in the Territory of Alaska with a lot of propaganda about how it might hurt the environment. Their real motives could have been, and probably were, something other than caring for some sparsely populated land that they knew little about and that could well have used some economic development.

Decades later, Californians fought oil development in an even more sparsely populated Alaskan area. This time they warned about what might happen to the poor, delicate caribou. It was easy to get people to join that bandwagon (another useful propaganda technique). As it turned out the caribou liked the warm pipeline and they multiplied more than ever and invaded the grazing lands of the reindeer that Eskimos were trying to herd. Regardless, the next time around the propagandists continued to use the caribou argument. That's another propaganda technique—if you keep repeating something long enough people will believe it. The whole Alaska-development issue was absurd in thinking people's minds.

> **Californian:** Why do you want a road to the north of your state?
>
> **Alaskan:** Well, we don't have a road to the north of our state.

We see here that propagandists have used environmental concerns, some real and some spurious, for a long time. Bringing the aura of science to an issue works for propagandists in other fields besides coal and oil—health for instance. Does vitamin C build immunity and help prevent colds? People have done "researches" using vitamin C too late and too little and, lo and behold, it does not cure colds—no mention of prevention. Now who makes money from those headlines? Maybe the manufacturers of cold medicines.

One evening a group of moms meeting at orchestra practice talked about the day's headlines that sugar does not make children hyper. This had the backing of "science" and even the backing of government, since it had paid for the study. To the credit of the moms, none of them believed the propaganda. Their own experience and common sense entered their thinking and overturned the "expert" scientists or "authoritative" government.

Euphemisms are used to propagandize that things are not as bad as it would sound if we used the straightforward word. Instead of *genocide* today, dictators are credited with *ethnic cleansing*. After World War I, soldiers came home shell-shocked. After World War II they had combat fatigue. Now they have post-traumatic stress disorder (PTSD). People are not addicted to drugs; they are chemical dependent. Children can begin noticing how propagandists choose words to affect the thinking of their readers.

Misquotes and misinformation are common. A current and common one is to argue that the constitution requires separation of church and state. This is heard so often that people on both sides of an argument believe it and use it to restrict religious expression of the people. But the first amendment of the constitution actually says, "Congress shall make no law respecting the establishment of religion, or prohibiting the free exercise thereof . . ." This restricts Federal law but does not restrict the people. Even states, as happened early in our history, could set up religious laws. But Congress could not.

A quick search on the Internet will bring up dozens of tricks of propagandists, and illustrations of them. This might be useful if you wish to pursue the topic in depth. It is a valuable language skill for your children to recognize propaganda in current issues swirling around them. The habits of daily thinking that children develop will go with them throughout life.

Family Thinking

Try keeping a list of thinking activities your family does that are not connected with lesson books. You could list games, conversations about cartoons or graphs or other items in media, analyzing ads, noticing propaganda. After you (or the children) list a few you will see that you have the thinking habit in your family or are building the habit, and you will not need to list any further.

Humors and IQs and Styles

Psychologists are always trying to analyze and label personality and thinking, but labels have limited usefulness. The Greeks labeled four humors—melancholic, choleric, sanguine, and phlegmatic. A century ago people's differences were called faculties. Charlotte Mason rejected that idea. Children were not bundles of faculties, she wrote. Mortimer Adler wrote that they are not bundles of reflexes, as the current "scientific" psychology purported.

Next, after the faculty psychology, came Lewis Terman and the "intelligence" psychologists. With lots of numbers and precision it looked scientific when they measured IQs. Everybody in those days was somewhere on the scale and got treated accordingly in school. High IQs did in fact predict high achievement in school, but with passing of time people saw that they did not necessarily predict success in life.

Next, came Howard Gardner who explained that the problem with IQ was that it included only two intelligences—verbal and logical-mathematical. Those two were used a lot in schools so naturally children with those two abilities achieved high in school. Gardner identified eight intelligences, and the IQ system faded from use. The new system helped teachers to value differences in children and not try to make everyone conform to heavy book learning. Differences, of course, are what everyone from the Greeks on down was trying to study. Today Gardner's system is most alive in David Lazear's training for adults in the business world.

For a time "brain-based" teaching became a fashion. Physiologists discovered some chemical and neurological happenings in the brain, and educators jumped to unwarranted conclusions. (Did they themselves need a course on thinking?) Physiologists found, for instance, a brain growth spurt at young teen age, so educators concluded they could pile on higher-level thinking at that time. But for physical growth spurts they do exactly the opposite, allowing children to grow through their "awkward" age.

Left-brain and right-brain differences became a fad in itself. Among other things, people taught that music uses the right brain and language uses the left brain. There is a bit of truth to that, but the more that people know about music the more they use both halves of the brain, even to listen. Educators wrote much about teaching to the "other" half of the brain. Are we to believe that God has left us floundering for these thousands of years using half our brains until modern science came along to tell us how to use the other half? The theories on teaching to the brain were premature and ineffective and now have faded from prominence.

Recently a molecular biologist, head of a brain research organization, spoke at a convention and explained that brain science does not currently have much to say to educators since nobody really knows how the brain works.

A new fashion now is styles, anywhere from four styles like the Greeks to thirty-two or more, depending on who you read. Some researchers name styles by personality types, some by strategies and preferences for studying, some by various ways of processing information in the minds, some by ways of giving out information, and some by ways of taking in information. Some believe their styles are built in permanently, others that they are flexible to one degree or another and can be learned.

With people mixing not only apples and oranges, but also pomegranates and guava, it is no wonder we cannot figure out how to label our children. Simple, some say. Boil down to *the* three perceptual styles: visual, auditory, and kinesthetic. Even those three do not sit still. People pull them apart or add to them. They say kinesthetic is whole body movement, so they add haptic, which is touch or grasp. They add olfactory, which is smell and taste. They add print. Now that is convenient. We do not have to decide, then, whether a preference for reading is visual or verbal or logical-sequential or independent or reflective or abstract. We can just say that a child likes to read.

Critics point out that researchers make extravagant claims based on their theories and not on their research. Some researchers promise that people will achieve better by using their system. One warns that learners will be harmed by not using his. There is no evidence, critics say, that matching teacher and learner styles has any positive effect on achievement. Actually nine studies do show positive effect, but nine others show a negative effect. The best we can say about those results is that styles must be only one among many learning factors and a minor one at that, not enough to tip the balance in those studies.

One researcher, Richard M. Felder, is surprised that people have made so much from his research. They have run away with it, doing far more than he intended. He has thirty-two styles in his system but has boiled them down to five pairs of opposites. An example of a pair is sequential-global. He explains that a teacher can easily teach to both. In other words, if you cannot diagnose a child or if you have both kinds in your group, you can describe the big picture first for the global learners and then go through the details, maybe wrapping up with the big picture again.

The researches thus far were not conducted on children anyway, but on university students or on managers and employees at businesses. Anthony F. Gregorc and others have cautioned against using their results with children. Felder's research involved university classes where lecture was the main method. He found lecture one of the most ineffective ways to teach, but he does not suggest dropping it. He would improve lectures by providing a short break within them wherein students with one or more partners must solve a problem. Just a small tweak like this helps. Homeschoolers do not have to worry much about lecture teaching, but this advice from a styles researcher shows that even he realizes that learning is not heavily dependent on styles. In the home we can tweak almost any curriculum in almost any way. Big tweaks if we want.

A thriving styles industry has arisen that sells diagnostic tests and offers advice based on inflated claims. One couple says their system is easy to use, but a teacher must take a week of training from them (at over $900, plus hotel costs) to learn how to use it.

A group of professors in the UK studied this whole field of styles research and concluded, "For more than forty years, hundreds of thousands of students, managers and employees have filled in learning style inventories, their scores have been subjected to factor analyses of increasing complexity, numerous learning styles have been identified, and what are the conclusions that stem from such intensive labour? We are informed that the same teaching method does not work for all learners, that learners learn in different ways and that teachers should employ a variety of methods of teaching and assessment. Comenius knew that and more in seventeenth century Prague and he did not need a series of large research grants to help him find out."[2] Homeschoolers, not so wordy as those scientists, also learn that their children differ without needing the researches to tell them.

In some countries children are categorized early in life and placed into educational tracks that then determine what they can do in the future. In America we try to leave more freedom. Bureaucrats do not set all student choices. We do not "play God" with their lives. A missionary pastor said that if he had followed his school counselor's advice he would be an accountant instead of a missionary.

Colonel David Stirling's early teachers had no idea what he would accomplish in the future. Gardner had not yet invented an interpersonal intelligence. Stirling didn't seem to have it anyway, and of other so-called leadership traits he showed none. He gained perseverance from overcoming a childhood speech impairment and illnesses. He left school and was climbing mountains when World War II began. He rushed home to Britain, signed up for war, and in time was injured in a parachute jump during desert fighting. The desert campaign was going badly and the British were considering retreat. Lying in a hospital Stirling thought up a better plan than the constant bombing.

After healing he used a bit of deception to get his idea to the British brass. He used his unnecessary crutches and hobbled to the gate of headquarters. Because he was a lowly lieutenant, sentries turned him away, so he hobbled off as though resigned to the No answer. Then at a gap in the fence he slipped through without crutches and fell in step with a group of senior officers going into the building. Just as a sentry shouted "Stop that man," he ducked into an office and surprised the deputy chief of staff for the Middle East.

Stirling said he was there on urgent business and proceeded to explain his plan for small assault units to attack enemy airfields behind the lines at night. This way they could do more damage than by the bombing. He spoke with confidence and the officer decided to let him try it. Most people sneered at the idea, but it would only take a few men. Let them be expendable.

So Stirling, the student with no leadership "faculties," recruited men and trained them and led them on the first of what Americans later would call special ops missions. They attacked by night and hid in the desert by day. In a few months they destroyed 250 enemy aircraft and countless vehicles and ammunition stashes. He was called the Phantom Major, even after advancement to colonel and knighthood to the Order of the British Empire.

What school counselor would have identified his particular bundle of faculties or styles and prepared Stirling for his great future?

Heart Thinking

Psychologists looking for bundles of faculties or intelligences miss completely the heart thinking the Bible tells about. Here are a few Bible statements about the heart. They show that the heart knows, considers, understands, thinks, believes, and has wisdom— when God puts it there.

> *Know* therefore this day, and *consider it* in thine heart, that the LORD he *is* God (Deuteronomy 4:39a).

Give therefore thy servant an *understanding* heart to judge thy people ... (I Kings 3:9a).

Who hath put *wisdom* in the inward parts? or who hath given *understanding* to the heart (Job 38:36)?

. . . that the *thoughts* of many hearts may be revealed (Luke 2:35b).

For with the heart man *believeth* unto righteousness (Romans 10:10a).

These are not isolated examples. Similar cognitive functions of heart are mentioned 243 times in the Bible. The moral and emotional and other uses of heart occur less often. Altogether the word *heart* appears 981 times and twenty-five percent of these refer to cognitive function. Not one of the 981 uses gives any hint of being figurative. We cannot dismiss the word that easily.[3]

When Christianity clashed with Greek philosophy many arguments ensued because of the two ways of thinking. Here are a few quotes from early Christians.

Thus, philosophers have reached the height of human wisdom, in understanding that which does *not* exist. But they have failed in attaining the power of saying what truly *does* exist (Lactantius, 7.44).

What indeed has Athens to do with Jerusalem? What agreement is there between the Academy and the church?... Away with all attempts to produce a mottled Christianity of Stoic, Platonic, and dialectic composition (Tertullian, 3.545)!

The philosophers are the patriarchs of all heresies (Tertullian, 3.482).

> . . . where is there any likeness between the
> Christian and the philosopher? Between the disciple of
> Greece and the disciple of heaven (Tertullian, 3.50)?

> Great is the error that the philosophers among
> them have brought upon their followers (Aristedes,
> 9.266).

The Greeks could not understand biblical thinking. They assumed that their system of logic, if followed carefully, would yield truth. By the second century three classes of philosophers developed—1) those who said they had found the truth, 2) those who said it is impossible to find truth, and 3) those who still searched for truth. Would you fit today's scientists into one of those categories?

Paul also participated in the clash of Greek thinking and Christian thinking. To illustrate, here are a few phrases from his letter to the Greek city of Corinth.

> The Greeks seek after wisdom: But we preach
> Christ crucified . . . unto the Greeks foolishness . . . it
> is written, I will destroy the wisdom of the wise . . . For
> the wisdom of this world is foolishness with God . . .
> your faith should not stand in the wisdom of men, but in
> the power of God (from 1 Corinthians 1—3).

We know little about the physiology of the brain's thinking and even less about the heart's thinking. Researchers today are becoming interested. Some have found that the heart "talks" to the brain via the vagus nerve, whereas people used to think only that the brain talks to the heart, telling it to beat faster or whatever is needed. They find, instead, that the heart can tell the brain to be on the alert as there may be danger ahead and it may have to respond extra quickly.[4] Some heart transplant patients take on characteristics from their donor.[5] Another researcher has found that a cranial nerve that goes to the voice box (larynx) surprises everybody by not going directly from brain to larynx. Instead, it drops lower, loops around the aorta near the heart, and then back up to the larynx.[6] *For out of the abundance of the heart the mouth speaketh* (Matthew 12:34b).

This heart thinking is a major reason that Christian homeschoolers succeed so well in life and in academic studies.

Curriculum for Thinking?

In the curriculum catalogs it is amazing how many descriptions of thinking books mention that they help children improve their test scores. Government money and testing these days drive education, and schools specifically teach for passing tests because they get more money if their children score higher. And what is in the thinking parts of the tests? Artificial bits of thinking that children can do with paper and pencil. That turns out to be a lot of analogies and things like sequence, opposites, and categories. With drawings or words or numbers, children must mark which comes next, which are opposite, and so on. In real life the youngest children can mate socks or sort silverware into the drawer. Older children can sort biographies, science, historical fiction, and other high-level categories. This real-life categorizing does not grow out of paper and pencil categorizing.

Students who work a practice book before a test do in fact score better on the test. They play that game to score as well as they can. But does it make them better thinkers in life? Not really. In one customer testimonial a parent wrote that her child scored well after using the curriculum. Then the following year his test score fell, so the third year she wanted him to use a thinking book again. This illustrates how poorly the skills transfer, as well as the artificial nature of this kind of testing. If the student had transferred the skills into life and into schools subjects, he would indeed have been a better thinker a year later at test time. This indicates that thinking does not work well as a separate subject. Students should practice thinking in every subject and in family life, too. We are preparing children for life, not for tests.

Your adult thinking is on a higher level than your children's, so you teach a lot just by conversing with them. Thinking is a language skill and one way to simplify your schooling is to let children think in content subjects and daily activities, and avoid spending too much time with courses on the latest trendy theories.

If any thinking books from publishers look good to you, try using them as enjoyable puzzle books to brighten your days. If these really engage your children's minds on their level, they will read the books even if you do not assign them for "thinking class."

Thinking courses for older students can succeed in educating *about* thinking processes. That is, students learn what syllogisms are, and logic, fallacies, analogies, inferences, and so on. This gives them names for procedures that they mostly use already if they grew up thinking about everything along the way. A college professor of reasoning teaches that formal logic, while needed for math and for programming computers, is inadequate to decide most controversial issues. Logic might also help for finding errors in the arguments of debates and of writings. Learning about syllogisms and such may be useful for college level and for interested high school students, but in itself it is not the route for children to become habitual thinkers. Thinking in all life situations and academic studies is the route.

6   Reading Skills

A beginning first-grade teacher on the opening day of school looked at her children with an inner fear. Could she teach them to read by the end of the year? With trepidation she began, doing mostly what the books told her to do and, yes, by the end of the year they could read the first grade readers, except for a couple of children, which is about the statistical norm for a class. In subsequent years she could face a new class with more confidence. She did not have to follow the book so closely and was guided more by the children themselves, by what they seemed to understand or not understand. She felt freer to try new ideas that she gleaned from colleagues and from teacher magazines. Constantly thinking about the teaching problems became a way of life for her—an enjoyable life of challenge and successes and a few unsolved problems along the way.

A few centuries earlier, Susannah Wesley and others like her taught their children letters. The word *phonics* and the phonics system were not used in those days. Mothers taught what historians now call the alphabet system of reading and, beginning with Genesis 1, showed their children how to read the Bible.

Colonial America still used the alphabet system. A school-book called *The New England Primer* taught the alphabet with rhymes like these.

A   In Adam's fall
        We sinned all.

B   Thy life to mend
        This Book attend.

In the 1800s William McGuffey, a professor of moral philosophy, wrote a series of school reading books primarily to teach moral lessons. These passed through several editions and sold by the millions, influencing the thinking of generations of Americans. He did not explain how to teach beginning reading. In his day children often learned to read first and then went to school. The "science" of phonics was being developed, and by the late 1800s eighth graders passed tests on phonics—items like trigraphs, diphthongs, orthography, cognate letters, prefixes, and many rules for spelling and syllabication.

Move forward to the early 1900s. Phonics teaching now began in the primary grades. A teacher on a beach one day heard children at play exclaiming, "Oh! Look, look!" "Run, Dick, run." She conceived the idea that children could learn to read more easily if the beginning textbooks were in their language, and she helped to produce the famous Dick and Jane readers, which used a highly structured system for beginning reading. In that day children arrived at school with little or no prior experience with colorful children's storybooks, so the textbooks began at that level—real beginning stuff like pointing to words and moving from left to right. After learning a few sight words in the pre-primer book, the children began to analyze them. What is the first letter? The last letter? What part of *run* is like *fun?* At primer level, they learned the sounds of practically all consonants, including details like hard and soft *c*. They learned suffixes like *er* and *ed*, the plural *s* ending, and families like *man, can, ran*. In the first grade book they learned consonant blends such as *st* and *fl*; numerous phonograms such as *wh, ow,* and *ight*; more suffixes; and compound words.

Through all this there was great emphasis on meaning. That's what reading was for—meaning. When a child was analyzing a word, he should make sure it fit into the sentence. There was no separation of learning to "read" first and learning to comprehend later. Reading *was* comprehension. Second graders continued phonics instruction to include everything that today's phonics zealots would like to see. Many generations of school children learned to read from Dick and Jane. Millions also learned what a happy life with family and friends could be. Today's phonics-first people caricature this as the look-say method, referring to only the few weeks of pre-primer instruction, the skills that parents now teach with colorful storybooks.

What will the future say about today's homeschool teaching? If they go by the commercial products touted in catalogs and magazines, they will say that we taught phonics first and reading later. They also will say we taught phonics earlier than ever before and more information than the children needed in order to read. They might also say we thought that reading consists of sounding out words, while comprehension is something else to teach and test for separately.

A Dick-and-Jane team member was asked in his later years whatever happened to Dick. "He became a politician. Run, Dick, run." Jane grew up and worked for women's rights. What will people say in the future about our "Dan had an ax and Dan sat on a van"?

In each historical period, people no doubt used a variety of methods. Who knows what Susannah Wesley told her children as they tried to read Bible words? Today there are many systems available and there is no need to stick with one formula through book after workbook after book. The real formula is not in the books. It is each child's unique growth. Instead of measuring progress artificially by pages covered in a book, we can relax from that daily frustration. Learning is not that linear. Months down the road or a semester down the road we will see how the children's reading has grown in many directions—like tree branches rather than in a single line.

Individual Tutoring

Tutoring is a common method in homeschooling, and it is the most effective method ever devised. While working with an individual child, it is easy to tell whether the work is within the child's ability. So homeschoolers need not waste time pressuring children to start too early or drilling them on too many phonics details. It works better to read from children's books and associate phonics with the stories.[1]

In an early reading stage, at the merging of read-aloud time and beginning reading lessons, a half-hour session may look like this.

1. The child reads two or three familiar books. Parent jots down any problems with particular words or letters.
2. Read yesterday's new book and work briefly on some of the words and letter sounds needed.
3. Try reading a new book. Help prepare the child by looking at the pictures together, identifying the characters, the little red hen or whomever. Point out an important word and talk about its first letter, or a part that is like a known word, or another feature that helps identify it. The reading itself can take many levels.

A high level is where the child reads it with help only on unknown words. A lower level is the parent reading one sentence and the child reading it after her, perhaps pointing to each word, similar to counting out squares on a game board—a one-to-one matching. Between those levels are taking turns, chorus reading together, the child reading repetitive parts that he knows, and any other system that mom and child like.

4. The child makes up a sentence about the book and the parent helps him write it, using any method appropriate to the child's current level. For instance, at an early level the parent could write each word on a separate small card, talking especially about one or two letters, and then the child assembles the sentence in order, with whatever help is needed. At a later level, the child himself writes the words, again with parent help as needed.

The power and efficiency of tutoring is that the parent follows the child's ability and interest rather than following a curriculum plan with its formula for learning skills in a certain order. When teaching phonics in context like this, there is no need for drill and kill. Even when drills are dressed up as songs and games, they become boring in time, but stories do not become boring. The parent should spend only a moment or two on any problem word or phonics pattern. If a child does not understand or remember, it will come up again later on. Use other cues besides just phonics and sounding out a word. The word must make sense in the sentence. In picture books, the picture can often help with figuring out the text. Meaning is uppermost. That is what reading is all about.

Parents who like record keeping could list books read and some phonics or new words learned in each one. (But many items will need re-teaching.) Parents who dislike detailed records could make a tape every month or two of the child reading, or just keep some of the observations made in step one above. Looking back on these should show progress. Records made occasionally show real progress. Day-by-day records of completed workbook pages are an artificial measure of progress.

Consonants and Vowels

People who do begin with phonics in spite of the real-book advice can make it easier by stripping it down to its bare bones. Strip off the three or four sounds of *a* and the rules for deciding which to use. Strip off the name of the letter and its position in the alphabet. The bare bones are to recognize it and to say /ă/ (the short sound) when you see it. This gets children going in the kind of readers that say the cat sat on a hat or Dan sat on a van.

A first grader who learned this way met up later with long *a*. He asked, "How do adults know when to say /ă/ and when to say /ā/?" "Well, sometimes they tell by the final *e* on the word." Actually adults do not go through that thinking, but Jimmy could for a while. It will work for *take* but not for *taking*. In the end he will have to use whatever sound works in a sentence, as you do for the vowels in *plead, bread,* and *break.* You just use the sound that works instead of searching through the rules you know for two vowels together and then selecting a rule and trying to apply it. But don't let a phonics zealot catch you letting Jimmy use context to decide. They think it's not legal to mix comprehension with phonics, and they malign the Dick and Jane readers for doing that.

Learning consonant sounds is easier than vowels because most of them have only one sound. Of the others only *c* and *g* have soft and hard sounds, the soft usually when followed by *y, i,* or *e* (exception, *get*). This is much simpler than the many complexities of vowels. Early Hebrew and other ancient languages had only consonants, no vowels. To try that in English, here is a little demonstration. The first line shows only vowels in a sentence and the second shows only consonants.

I u a I u a I o ou ou-e o.

ll hff nd ll pff nd ll blw yr hs dwn.

Consonant reading works so well that older students can use it as shorthand for many words when they must take rapid notes. For beginning reading it may be more important than vowels.

One mother owned three phonics programs and asked what others she should buy so as to have everything. She was already overloaded. Another mother was shopping for new phonics because her second grader did not like the program they had. He already was reading, and after two consultants advised her to drop formal phonics lessons she gained enough confidence to do so. Her son then was happier and had more time to read, and reading is the end result we seek, not phonics expertise.

Most parents feel they must have a day-by-day, step-by-step formula for teaching reading. Lesson books are arranged with this kind of formula and that gives a feeling of daily progress—at least progress through the books. But parents learn to speed along or creep through books as fits their children. For instance, the cat-sat-hat system works so easily at first that children can begin at younger ages than with other systems. Then after the consonant-vowel-consonant (cvc) pattern of *sat* and *sit,* they arrive at the ccvc pattern of *trap* and *spin.* This blending requires further mental development so some children reach their limit at this point, and they must wait awhile before continuing in the formula book.

Any and all reading systems have worked in history past and can work today with the vast majority of children. We can begin with the cat sat on a hat or with the big bad wolf huffing and puffing. We should not push unduly, but follow the lead of the children and tell them what they need when they need it.

Purpose for Reading

Once children can read little storybooks, reading can disappear as a separate subject. It is now a skill to *use,* not a subject to learn. Use it for enjoyment a lot at first. Use it for learning history and other subjects, as children grow older. Use it for character building by reading about heroes and other good role models. Use it for building Christian life attitudes. One mother liked to see her four daughters reading Christian romances because she wanted them to make Christian marriages themselves. And they all did.

What about giants and monsters and violence? When children read these or listen to you read, they make images in their heads and these are images they can handle. If they watch the same on TV or video they see someone else's images, often too frightening and too much to handle. In the old tales, the dragons and monsters were the "bad guys" and good won out in the end. The old tales, many called "fairy tales," have been handed down from time unknown, probably since the population dispersion at Babel, changing gradually over the centuries. Why are there giants in the stories? This could be mankind's memory of real giants that the Bible says lived before the Flood and again after it. Why are there dragons? These are mankind's memory of dinosaurs that did in fact live concurrently with humans. The dinosaur name is a recent invention. What about elves, dwarfs, gnomes, and other fantastic creatures? These could well be memories of demon contacts. People turned them into lovable creatures, just as many do today with the so-called aliens from outer space: "They are here to help us."

Why does a handsome prince come to take away his bride? These stories are obvious parallels to Christ and His church. These tales, too, began long ago.

Some families decide that their children should read none of the old tales but should be raised on Bible stories instead. You naturally should raise your children on Bible stories, and as to whether or not you add at times some old tales you must follow your heart. Many new stories are like Harry Potter, reversing long tradition by turning the wizard into the protagonist, the one the reader identifies with, instead of making him the bad guy who loses in the end.

Reading for pleasure and reading for knowledge are almost the same thing, as you see when your children enjoy biographies and other non-fiction. Some children easily become "readers" and you need only take them to the library or even select a pile of books yourself and say, "Here, read these in the next two weeks." Other children for various reasons will spend their lives on mechanical or mathematical or other matters that require less reading. Encourage their talents and also encourage as much reading as you can by finding topics that interest them.

After beginning gently with children's books, you can continue reading instruction in all reading and every subject rather than in a special "reading class." Learn science vocabulary from the science book, place names from the geography book, Bible vocabulary from the Bible, and so on. That is more efficient than isolating the skills in a separate class and then trying to transfer them to where they are needed. Think of reading as a skill to use everywhere.

Speed-Reading

One result of reading aloud a lot is that children tend to become slow, word-by-word readers. This is the speed of speech, about 200 to 300 words per minute. Students can at least double that speed by a few days of practicing this system. Choose easy material. Lay a card above the line you are reading and slide it downward at a speed that pushes you a little. Cover each line before mentally pronouncing the last word or phrase. Your eyes saw it. Keep going. Try not to pronounce mentally, but just get the thought. Observe the rule that you never go back to check on something you think you missed. In most cases you did not miss it, and knowing you can't go back heightens your concentration to think and to catch it the first time. Because of heightened concentration, this speed is good to use for material that you must learn and must answer questions on. It will not work, of course, for material packed with new words and complex concepts.

Some books on speed-reading contain passages with words already counted and with questions at the end. This helps you to figure words per minute and to check on whether you really got the content—"comprehension," to use the jargon. In this case the question is not whether you comprehend the concepts, but whether you caught what the passage said. Without a speed-reading book, students could use the same system with material you have already. Try a younger sibling's textbook that has questions. Count the words in ten lines and calculate the average words per line to use in estimating. After this initial work, calculating words per minute becomes easy. Read the questions ahead of time, as this helps concentration, and it is good practice for tests like SAT.

After students reach the speed of 600 to 800 or more words per minute, do they want to proceed to thousands per minute? In any college speed-reading class many students do in fact achieve that by practicing a technique of moving their eyes rhythmically in a rolling pattern down a page, a few seconds per page. This way they can get the gist of a story. But then most of them report that they do not enjoy the story. They want to go slower and savor the events and emotions. This speed might do for the night before a literature test. So would a Cliff Notes summary.

The ads about "learning" at those fast speeds are false. Moving the eyes faster does not move the brain faster. Thinking occurs at all speeds. Speed itself does not affect how much learning occurs except in the one instance where a word-by-word speed allows the mind to wander, and a somewhat faster speed avoids that. Skim reading serves some purposes. Slow, reflective reading serves other purposes. Speeds in between are useful too. Students gain by having several kinds available. They should not read everything at the speed of speech.

Follow-Up

A common question is "What about book reports?" In classrooms a book report is just that—a brief writing to report to the teacher that a student read the book. He must tell why he liked the book, who the characters were, and a few matters to prove he read it. You saw the child sitting around reading the book so you do not need proof. Thus you do not need the schoolish book report for every book. But it is a good idea to follow up on some books in some ways. The suggestions below may spark some ideas for doing this. Some involve writing and some involve speaking.

Listing and categorizing. As soon as children understand the difference between fiction and non-fiction they could list their books under the two categories. Later, expand the categories to books about Bible, history, creation science, other science, and any other categories and subcategories you wish. To help themselves remember what is in a book, the children could write a few words, not necessarily a sentence, such as "about exploring all the way to the Pacific."

Categorizing books involves understanding the categories, evaluating a book, and deciding its category. Writing an eight-word summary involves quite high level thinking. And looking back on the list is insightful. If a girl has read nothing but horse stories recently, you may wish to say as one mother did, "You have to read two other books before you read another horse story."

A growing list is motivating in itself, and looking back on it helps children see that they are accomplishing something. Unless we point this out to children, they ordinarily do not notice the achievements of a month or other period. Their time frame of thinking is too short.

Conversing and speaking. Speaking is a language skill, and along with reading it forms two-way communication. Reading takes in information and speaking gives out information. That is why curriculums so often follow up reading with discussion questions to promote talking about the selection. But the questions and issues that children raise are better triggers for learning and thinking than the book questions. Research has confirmed that. So your informal family conversation is more powerful.

It often is difficult to draw out conversation about a book immediately after a child finishes reading it, before he has time to think much and digest it. Cooperative children will answer your questions, and your observations about the book can promote his thinking about it. But the best conversation starters are those that come from the children themselves.

Your fifth grader brings *The Monitor and the Merrimac* and says, "Here, you have to read this," and you do have to read it because in his excitement he needs someone to agree with him about the book. After you read it, you two could talk about the one book or relate it to other Civil War books or other sea books. Such conversation promotes the skills of reviewing, evaluating, and thinking about the book.

Your seventh grader brings *Winnie the Pooh* and says, "This is good! You should read it." Your first thought might be that she is too old for that kid's story, but you haven't read it so you had better do so and see what captured her mind. You find out that it's not strictly a kid's story because it takes at least a seventh grader to understand some of the humor, and you become impressed with the cleverness of the author. Soon you read parts to the whole family. For years afterward some family member will say "He talks just like Eeyore" or "That sounds like something Pooh Bear would do." This extended conversation bonds your family together by one more story.

Teenage Randy took to reading science fiction. His mom thought, "Oh no. I've got to lead him to something more biblical, something more wholesome than that." But she ended up reading a couple of books at his insistence, and they spent long, late evenings in deep intellectual conversations. This was better than any thinking course she could have assigned. Those sci-fi writers could certainly raise stimulating what-if questions, much like creative scientists do in their work. (Many imaginative books today are classified as science fantasy instead of science fiction.)

Some families use a straightforward assignment to tell back the information. One mom reading about this narration technique pleaded with her group for help. "My son and I have always talked about the books we read, but it doesn't seem formal enough." A sensible mom responded, "If your son talks about the books, he *is* narrating." How right! That boy was using a life skill of communicating about books and ideas. Why should he regress to an artificial schooling format?

Writing. Like speaking, writing is a way to converse with a book. Students must think and process in their minds what it says and respond in writing. One idea is book reviews (not school reports). A review can be a teaser that aims to persuade people to read the book. Your homeschool newsletter or church newsletter might use a good review of a book in their library. Another kind of review explains the message of a book so people can learn it without reading the whole book. Francis Bacon said that some books are to be swallowed and digested, and "Some books also may be read by deputy, and extracts of them made by others." Reviews in magazines often are deputy reports with added critique by the reviewer. This forms an essay response. An older student could try giving the message of a book and then comparing it with the Bible.

Many children enjoy telling a story from a new viewpoint. How would the Good Samaritan story sound as told from the view of the wounded victim or from one of the three passersby? What story would the colt tell who was untied by strangers and then carried Jesus into Jerusalem? After reading a dozen horse stories, Susie may want to write a horse story of her own.

It is important to find audiences because writing is communicating *to* somebody. Observe the caution about not turning everything into penmanship practice, also a caution about not requiring writing or follow-up on every book. Much of children's reading is gathering information, with thinking and talking along the way. The hard work of writing comes after a mind is filled with something to write about.

Checklist for Reading Follow-Up

This list can help you keep track of what you have tried and what you would like to try in the future.

1. List of books read:
   begun _____ growing _____
2. Number of list categories:
   two _____ more _____ (name them)
3. Converses about books:
   reluctantly _____ with pleasure _____
4. Narrates book information:
   fair _____ good _____
5. Writes book information:
   fair _____ good _____
6. Writes essay-type critique:
   fair _____ good _____

Reading Problems

The labels ADD and ADHD are nothing more than names for symptoms—behaviors. You notice these behaviors so someone says you must have a professional diagnosis. The psychologist has lists of the behaviors, and if your child exhibits a given percentage of these he diagnoses that, yes, your child *has* the condition.

Before going to a psychologist, try for two or three months to completely eliminate all prepared foods and boxed mixes with their long lists of chemical ingredients. Eat plain, natural foods—fruits and vegetables; meats and eggs; and whole, unrefined grains. Also eliminate or greatly reduce sugar. Allow no soft drinks. The artificially sweetened ones are worse than the sugared ones. Make lemonade with Stevia, a natural sweetener that at this writing is deemed safe. Use only whole-grain, unsweetened cereals. Buy fruits and juices with no sugar added. You could help your busy schedule by including this work in your schooling. Let children read grocery labels and nutrition articles and talk with you about the information. Assign them the home economics task of cooking things "from scratch."

Children who do not respond to this nutrition treatment may have some kind of hormonal imbalance, and what are currently called "alternative" doctors may test for that and treat with natural nutrition supplements. Drugs should be a last resort, if used at all.

A different kind of problem is crossed-dominance, and this affects about ten percent of children. Refer to the Appendix for information about that.

The nutrition regimen should help with about half of today's learning difficulties. Kevin never was cured of his hyperactivity. He spent summers digging a fishpond, caring for horses, and other vigorous activities. As soon as he was old enough, he joined the volunteer fire department and was on call for accidents and all kinds of emergencies, as well as fires. He loved the pager calling him any hour of the day or night. Any community needs a few people like Kevin.

7 Study Skills

Recently the topic of study skills became an urgent subject in many public school districts. Surveys and tests showed that children were shamefully poor in these important skills, so schools added a separate course, trained teachers specifically for this, and thus an overcrowded curriculum grew more crowded.

Educators know that a better way is for the civics teacher to teach children how to read civics texts and the science teacher to help students learn the unfamiliar words. Anybody could tell them to organize their papers in a binder and to keep track of assignments. But nobody does. Each teacher hopes the students arrive in her class with the skills they need for it.

Homeschoolers have the advantage of teaching everything, or at least overseeing everything, and being able to infuse study skills right into the content where they are needed. The children, then, do not need to transfer a skill learned in "skills class" over into the science or math class where they need to use them. That kind of transfer does not work well.

Though study skills do not require a separate class, they are important. Below are described some useful skills to teach—in the content subjects, of course. As children become proficient in the techniques they can take more and more responsibility for their own learning.

Manage the Study Environment

You think your older children are settled for a while with their work and the toddler is OK for now, so you call your fourth grader for his arithmetic lesson. What happens? Does he scramble around finding his book and paper, and then has to sharpen a pencil? And he forgot where the problems are that he is supposed to show you today? Look at this as a teaching situation, not a discipline situation—not yet anyway. See that he has his own shelf or drawer space, notebook, and supplies. Explain to him how to organize these details, and explain that this is part of being a good student.

This simple organizing is a basic study skill. Older children with projects longer than day-by-day assignments need more advanced organizing skills. Do they know how to break large projects into smaller parts and schedule the parts so they can finish in time? At home they may not always have deadlines such as the science fair date, but they will later, in college or the work world. So they can learn to set goals, to estimate how long the work will take, and learn to manage their time. Children should know that good time management is part of being good students.

Do your children know the environment that helps them study best? Some need quiet isolation. Some study better with people around them. Some like music playing and can mentally ignore it while studying. Musicians' minds tend to focus on the music and become distracted from other tasks. (Radio advertisers lose that portion of their audience by using background music.) Does your child really accomplish more with the music? You may have to experiment a little and see how good a report she can write while music plays. A technique for students to use when feeling stuck on a difficult problem is to leave it for a few moments. Play through a piano piece or practice on just two troublesome measures. Run around the house a few times or jump rope for five minutes. Then return to the study task. Older students stuck on rewriting an important paper could let it rest for a day or two and then tackle it again.

Some students' peak energy is in the morning; others' may be later. Children could work on the most difficult subject at that peak time. You, unfortunately, cannot usually adjust your schedule that way. We adults have learned to sublimate things like that while we do what must be done.

Some other aspects of good student life are proper sleep, nutrition, and exercise. These are largely in your control, but help your children to know that these all help their learning. These health matters contribute to managing stress, and stress interferes with learning.

Another non-stress factor is self-concept and positive outlook on life. When teachers first learned this they went overboard with constant compliments. "Oh, that's great, Kevin. You're doing a good job, Rose. I like that." On and on a steady stream of self-concept boosting filled especially the preschool and kindergarten rooms. This attitude led to the strange situation where American students' math achievement was lower than practically all nations that participated in international testing. Yet American students thought they were great in math. Those teachers with too many compliments thought self-concept would help learning, but actually it is learning that helps self-concept.

Children should recognize when they need help and should feel free to ask for it. This, too, is a skill, and it alleviates stress they may have in facing a difficult subject. Most important in managing stress is to develop a good spiritual and moral viewpoint. These actually appear on secular lists of study-skill factors that help to develop better students with higher achievement. These and other positive life attitudes and good motivation play a large part in the high achievement of homeschoolers.

Checklist for Study Environment Skills

1. Keeps books and supplies organized.
   Sometimes ____ Usually ____
2. Uses study time without delay and waste.
   Sometimes ____ Usually ____
3. Cooperates cheerfully with family health practices.
   Sometimes ____ Usually ____
4. Shows realistic assessment of self.
   Sometimes ____ Usually ____
5. Appears motivated to learn.
   Sometimes ____ Usually ____

Checklists in this book can provide a quick reminder of the information in the preceding section, or when you wish you can use some of them to actually check off the skills of one or more of your children.

Dictionary and Reference Skills

Before tackling dictionary skills the children need to know the alphabet in order. Common practice is to teach alphabetic order as early as age three or four, but when you stop to think about it, you see there is no need for that until around grade three when a dictionary becomes useful for children. At that time you could give specific lessons on dictionaries, as suggested below. Afterward, infuse this skill with subjects whenever there is need to look up a word. This infusion system develops lifelong habits of using the dictionary.

Alphabetizing. About third grade age teach alphabetizing in the order shown below. Repeat each step until the child does it proficiently before moving on to the next step.

1. Alphabetize a list of about six words that each begin with a different letter. Use names of friends and family, of foods, or other items interesting to the children.
2. Alphabetize a short list beginning with the same letter, but with different second letters.
3. Alphabetize about four words beginning with the same two letters but with different third letters. (From the top of your head you can make a list of four *st* words: stop, step, stiff, string. Do four *br* words or *cl* words and so on by just trying a different vowel with each.)

A child who can do step 3 easily should understand the whole system and you need not practice alphabetizing by more and more letters. If a child struggles too much with these assignments, wait for two months or four months and try again. When he is mentally ready it will take some thought but not be unduly difficult.

After a child has a little experience with alphabetizing from the three steps above, begin to apply that knowledge to the dictionary. Use thinking methods, not mindless methods. For example, to look up *eclipse,* a child can consider for a moment where to open the dictionary to come close to the letter *e.* Then with the dictionary lying open, he should think again whether he must go backward or forward and how far. He turns a batch of pages that seems about right. Continue this procedure until he locates *eclipse.* The goal is to think about each move, not to see how fast the child can do it.

Use the mind and move slowly. In time sufficient speed will come without even trying. While using the mind, children will not hate looking up words.

Guide words. After children know how to look up words, show them the "shortcut" of using guide words at the top of dictionary pages. Give the word *pyramid* and have them try to open a dictionary at the letter *p,* as before. They may have to turn forward or backward a couple of times to get there. Then notice how the guide words tell the first and last words on the page. Would *pyramid* fit between those? If not, would *pyramid* be forward or backward from here? Turn a clump of pages all at once to try to get close. Look at the guide words again and see if *pyramid* will fit. You might turn to the correct page yourself, or close to it, and let the child check the guide words.

The word *pyramid,* or whatever word you have selected, may be enough for one day's lesson. Other days try more words from children's history or science reading. This one-at-a-time practice with words that children need to know in their schoolwork helps them to see the usefulness of dictionaries. Moreover, the children will have learned to use their minds. Do not move on to page-tearing, speed races. That develops sloppy guesswork. After the few lessons described above, you can quit being picky about the details. The children now will use their minds more while looking up words, and they need not be slaves to the details of the procedure you taught.

Finding a word efficiently is a third or fourth grade task. Teens can move on to understanding some of the information given in the dictionary for each word. What part of speech is it? Or can it be used, say, as either an adjective or noun? Which of its several meanings are you using now? Etymology: Did this word come from Latin or French or elsewhere? And derivations: Is it Floridians or Floridans? Learning just one item on one word when it is needed builds awareness of the information that can be gleaned from dictionaries—more in adult dictionaries than in simplified children's dictionaries. Sometime read front matter in your dictionary and find interesting information that most people never read. Help your children see the dictionary as a friend and helper.

The Bible and phone book. Use the same principles you used for dictionaries to teach how to find verses in the Bible or names in the phone book. Teach children to think about their moves: "Let's see; that's in Paul's letters—Romans, First and Second Corinthians . . ." They need to know the books from memory, just as they know the alphabet.

In phone books children need to know about the business, government, and residential listings; and how to use the yellow pages differently from the white pages. Guide words help just as they do in the dictionary. Children can learn most of these skills in life situations if you take advantage of them. When you or a child needs a number, help the child through the thinking processes to find it. A few such real-life experiences, maybe only one or two, are all that most children need to become proficient at using phone books.

Guide words are usually on the spines of encyclopedias, so children can select the volume they need with only one try. Other kinds of reference books, including grammar books, may be on your shelves, and as need arises children can become acquainted with how to use these various references.

Checklist for Reference Study Skills

1. Can recite the alphabet. ____
2. Can alphabetize by one letter ____
   two letters ____ three letters. ____
3. Can use guide words. ____
4. Can recite the books of the Bible. ____
5. Can use phone books independently. ____

Textbook Reading Skills

Textbook reading includes all kinds of informative materials—textbooks, encyclopedias, articles, pamphlets, and non-fiction books. The study skills described here are for children beyond beginning reading. Students can work on these reading study skills from about fourth grade and up, even through college.

One level of reading is called *surface reading* or *surface learning*. A student using surface learning memorizes facts and details, learns one thing at a time in order, and may not manage to fit them together into an overall picture. Children start out this way, but they should move on to *deep learning*. A student using deep learning tries to understand meaning behind the facts. He relates ideas. For example, he considers the evidence given and decides whether a conclusion is justified, or he organizes a sequential picture of events.

It has become an American trait to extend "reading classes" all through the grades to try to teach these deep-level skills. But it is better to do this in a science or government or other content class. This is a more efficient curriculum plan. If your schedule is not cluttered with skills classes, you can progress farther in content classes.

We can categorize reading study skills in the order they are performed, showing what a student should do before, during, and after a textbook assignment:

1. Pre-reading survey
2. Reading a section with active mental processing
3. Post-reading review

Many skills are included in each of the above categories, so children need enough time to learn and practice each skill. Following are a few ideas for doing this, with parts worded as you might instruct the student.

1. Pre-reading. For these lessons, choose a text on science, geography, civics, or another subject. This system works on most non-narrative, information-filled books. Begin by examining the book's structure. Look at the table of contents and decide what this book is going to teach you. Look in the back and see if there is a glossary, index, or other helps. You may need these later, so it is helpful to know what is there.

Now look at the structure of the first chapter. It has a chapter title and probably subheadings. From the chapter title what do you think you will learn? Does the chapter have questions at the end? Read them. Does it have vocabulary words at the end or beginning? Read and learn them if there are not too many to learn all at once. Does the chapter have a summary? Read it.

This may be enough for one lesson, depending on the book and on the child. The best way to teach all this is orally as a tutor. Lead a child through each activity and question in these instructions and have him tell you the answers.

2. Reading. For the next lesson, read the chapter title and say again what you will learn from this chapter. Read the first subheading and turn it into a question. For example, "Everyday Life in Rome" becomes "How did the ordinary people live?" The first time you may need to form the question yourself. This models for the child how to turn a heading into a question. Then the child should write the question on a sheet of notebook paper. Divide the sheet by drawing a vertical line down the center. Write the question on the left and save the right side for the answer.

Now read the section and tell the answer to the question. Do not write the answer yet; save that for later. Repeat this lesson procedure for each following section until you finish the chapter. Take as many days as needed.

Help the child become adept at making questions from the subheadings. Collect each question in the left-hand column of the notebook sheet. For books with short chapters and no subheads you can treat each chapter that way; write a chapter question in the left column.

3. Post-reading. Review the chapter now by seeing if you remember an answer for each question in the notebook. Here, again, you can model for the child. Explain your thinking as you form direct and clear answers to the questions. Answers need not be what we call "complete sentences." It is grammatically OK to write answers just as we would speak them. Sometimes the student may have to check back and reread a section. After you and the child decide on a good answer, write it in the right-hand column. If a child has manual writing difficulties, you could write the answers, or some of them, to stay focused on thinking about the content and avoid getting bogged down with the handwriting. When all questions are answered, look back over the answers to see how this helps you review for a test, or helps to show your learning of the chapter.

Ask now a very important question: *Do you know this chapter better than if you had just read it through?* If the student can look back in this way and realize what he has learned, he is monitoring, or checking on, his own learning. This is a valuable skill, perhaps the most valuable study skill he can acquire.

If there is a chapter summary, you could use that for another kind of review. If there are chapter questions you can use those too. Pre-arranged chapter questions seem to work well for adults but not so well for children. The questions a child makes from the subheadings work better.

On subsequent chapters repeat the chapter pre-reading, then the reading, and the post-reading review. The child should become more adept at surveying the chapter, at turning the headings into questions, and at using his questions later for review by writing the answers. Back off from helping as the child becomes more able to do these activities independently. Later, even without using every step, students will always read books more attentively because of the lessons you gave on these steps. All future learning will be enhanced.

More Reading Skills

After a student becomes proficient in the style of study reading described above, provide lessons on alternative skills. Some skills are explained briefly below, and for good results use the same lesson plans as above. That is, at first you do it with the child, modeling your thinking. Continue lessons through a whole chapter or several chapters until the child learns the new style of study reading.

One style is to **highlight** or underline key words or portions that will facilitate review. Begin by noting the section heading. Turn it into a question as before, or at least anticipate what you should learn from the section. That helps for deciding what parts are significant to highlight, and that act of deciding is the critical element here, not the highlighting itself. The idea is to get the student to process the material in his own mind. Discuss and work alongside the child while he learns this highlighting system. Model your thinking by explaining why you select the words you do. Let the child explain his choices. The bold words in this section provide one example of what highlighting can do. Do one or two sections per day, and after you finish a chapter, review it by reading back through the headings and the highlighted portions. Again, ask the important question: *Do you know this chapter better than if you had just read it through?* Let the child study more chapters by the highlighting method so he gains proficiency in using this method. If you highlight books that you own, you can look at them years later and quickly review what is in them.

The method of **taking notes** works with children old enough to write easily. It particularly helps children whose attention tends to stray; they can take notes after every paragraph or other short portion of reading. Notes are paraphrases, or putting important information into your own words. This requires mentally reorganizing the information, not just copying something from the text. If the text is mostly facts and simple information then the highlighting method is a better study skill to use. Students can learn to decide if note taking is an appropriate method for the text they must study, or if another method would work better. After reading and taking notes, review by reading back through the notes, and ask again: *Do you know this chapter better than if you had just read it through?*

Outlining is based on a level of thinking where students can identify major ideas and sub-ideas to go under them. If their thinking is on that level, then learning the format of the As and Bs with numerals indented under each is comparatively easy. Just looking at somebody's outline can teach that. If you want your student to outline something, attack the project at the thinking level, not just the level of learning outline formatting. Help him identify the major ideas and then some sub-ideas related to each. One good use for an outline is for speaking. After a student outlines some book information, he can use the outline to speak before the family or another group. Or he could use it to write a summary of the book material. Teachers consider outlining to be difficult to teach. It is hard work because of the thinking involved.

Graphic organizers accomplish the same effect as outlining but are simpler for some people. These can take any shape a student might invent to help him see what is in the text. Show a chain of events by connecting them in a line, either vertically or horizontally. Show a family tree to organize who is related to whom. A spider map shows a main item in the center and several lines reaching outward with a label on each. Then horizontal lines with sub-labels can be connected to those. Students who learn a bit about graphic organizers for a reading assignment can later use them even more productively for their writing. One teen resisted at first because it looked like more writing to do, and he already had too much swarming around in his mind. Nevertheless, he and his mother selected a graphic style from Internet samples, and he found that it helped him handle the swarm of ideas.

Writing **summaries** is a high-level study skill that you can work on occasionally through the years. To work on a summary, a student must first study the material by highlighting or any of the previously described study methods. Next, he must identify which are important general concepts, not low-level details. Then he must organize the concepts into a written summary. Children can begin learning this after they write well, maybe sixth grade or later, and by upper level high school be able to write good summaries.

In all the study skills mentioned here, you can see that the main idea is for students to *do* something mentally with the text beyond passively reading it. They must mentally process material in some way for it to move from what psychologists call short-term memory into long-term memory. Then the post-reading review serves to set the information more firmly in memory and make it more retrievable.

The study skills described here require intense work, so sprinkle the teaching throughout the grades, sometimes with a bit here and a bit there, and sometimes with a unified set of lessons as described. Children should read numerous books with various levels of intensity. After practicing the skills here, they will be better able to choose an appropriate reading style for their purpose with each book.

Checklist for a Child's Reading Study Skills

1. Pre-reading:
   Knows how to become acquainted with all parts of a book. ____
2. Reading:
   a. Can turn headings into questions, and then read and tell the answers. ____
   b. Can highlight significant words. ____
   c. Can take good notes of significant ideas. ____
   d. Can write summaries.

   　　fair ____ good ____

3. Post-reading:
Can review his work and monitor his learning. ____

Memory Skills

The whole method. We have a peculiar situation concerning memory in that all the world ignores the best known method and uses less effective ones. At least that is true in our Christian world of Bible memory. The best system is called the "whole" method. We know it is best through research that began in the early 1900s. Education research was the scholarly thing to do in those days, and memory was easy to measure. So people researched over and over all aspects of memorizing they could think of until they fairly exhausted the topic and moved on to others. Through all that effort we learned that the whole memory system is easier, takes less time, and achieves smoother recitation and longer retention.

Children can use the whole method to learn valuable Bible passages. They can memorize also from the Declaration of Independence, the preamble to the Constitution, Lincoln's Gettysburg address, and any number of poems and literary passages that will enrich your children's lives and thinking.

To begin trying the whole method, first set up the environment for it. If you can manage family devotions regularly, that is an ideal setting for memorizing Bible. Otherwise choose a meal that you share together. Car time works for some families, or another time in the school day.

Choose a psalm or other passage such as John 1:1–5. On the first day, you simply read through the passage together. Those who read may use their Bibles. Children who do not read follow as best they can, listening or saying some parts as they trail along behind. That is all for day one. The following days are similar. The goal is that in three months or so all who are old enough will know the passage by heart. The younger children gain in many ways, even though they may not memorize it all.

As you recite each day, the reading children will gradually quit following in their Bibles. You may need to suggest that they look up from their Bibles when they can. Occasionally you might check that a child correctly pronounces a word like *comprehended.* Answer questions the children have about meaning, but it is not necessary to carry on a unit of study on the passage. Some books for Sunday school teachers said, "Be sure the children understand the verse before they memorize it." This is useless advice for Scripture memory. (It works for multiplication tables, though.). When does any of us fully understand a Scripture? Children can just as well memorize first and learn the meaning more fully during the rest of their lives.

Continue reciting daily until you have not just learned a passage, but overlearned it. Then review on a diminishing schedule. For instance, for one or two months recite the passage once a week (instead of the new passage you are starting to learn). Then review once a month. Eventually, once a year will be sufficient. There is no specific rule about this schedule. The length of a passage, the amount of overlearning and other variables all affect this, so adjust as you see a need for more review or less. The principle of a diminishing need for review continues to apply.

If your family learns three or four passages a year—or even just two—these add up to considerable Scripture for your children to carry in their hearts wherever life may take them—to legislative halls or to enemy prison camps, to their future families or to fellow workers. After some passages of six or fewer verses, your family may feel brave enough to tackle a longer passage, perhaps a full chapter. Many teenagers have learned whole Bible books.

Use this whole method for poems and other items as well as for Scripture. To review, four phases of this process are:

1. Read and recite the whole passage many times.
2. When the passage is almost memorized spend extra work on any remaining hard parts.
3. Continue reciting until the passage is overlearned.
4. Review on a diminishing schedule.

When you are just starting to use this method, it helps to remind yourself that research shows that the whole method of memorizing: 1) takes less total time and 2) produces better memory results. Children will recite more smoothly and remember longer. They will not stop between verses and try to remember which comes next; they just recite on through as they recite through the alphabet. Give this a good try without reverting to the familiar verse-by-verse method.

Language features that help memory. Research has shown that children memorize the King James Bible more easily than other versions. This news surprises most people, but the reasons for this are the cadence, or rhythm, of the English language. John Wycliffe worked on cadence in his second version and William Tyndale followed that plan, insisting that his Bible be suitable for reading aloud. The King James translators likewise considered how the Bible would sound in public reading. They spent two years working on cadence. Compare these lines.

> *The Lord is my shepherd;*
> *I shall not want.* (KJV)

> *The Lord is my shepherd,*
> *I shall lack nothing.* (a modern version)

The King James sentence ends with the stressed word *want*, while the other ends with an unstressed syllable—noth*ing*—which is weaker cadence. As to meaning, *want* is not outdated. A dictionary gives this example: She would never allow her parents to want. Do more young children know *lack* than know *want?* What looks at first glance like a simple word change is not so simple after all. It gains nothing in meaning, and it loses power in its cadence.

Power in English language comes from its rhythm, which also aids memory, and which applies to prose and not only poetry. Short words help the rhythm. The King James Bible contains 250 percent more one-syllable words than longer words. Latin with all its inflections could not have such impressive cadence. Tyndale said that English language agrees with the Hebrew one thousand times more than Latin does. He also concluded that English captures the quality of New Testament Greek better than Latin does.

Further in this psalm, some versions change *still waters* to *quiet waters* or to *still and restful waters*. Again, it gains nothing in meaning and it loses in rhythm and sound. Linguists explain that progressing from a short vowel in *still* to a longer vowel in *waters* contributes to the calm effect. Also the harsh *q* of *quiet* intrudes on the calmness. This same vowel progression, along with consonant alliteration, is in the *still small* voice Elijah heard. Recent versions change that to a *gentle whisper* or *sound of a gentle blowing*.

These are a few language reasons why the King James Bible is easiest to memorize. It would also prepare your children for Shakespeare and other literature. Whatever version you decide to use, your family will be richer for following a tradition of memorizing. Imagine what this can add to future family reunions. Young grandchildren can join or listen with awe as you all recite Bible passages together.

Chunking. Another fact that longtime research has reported is that people can hold in their short-term memory seven items plus or minus two. Most phone numbers we use have seven digits, and that is the average memory span. We can hold those in our minds long enough to dial them, and then we lose the numbers unless we think more and process them some way to move them into long-term memory. A helpful secret that few people use is to "chunk" the numbers. For instance, 145-6412 recited digit by digit is seven items to remember. But "one forty-five" becomes one item or two depending on whether or not you visualize it as a number in the hundreds. Sixty-four twelve easily becomes two chunks, so seven items is reduced to just three or four, and the number is easier to remember. Looking for patterns also helps memory, as noticing the sequence of 4, 5, 6 in the above number. Some children will prefer spatial thinking, and memorize how the movements proceed on the touch-tone buttons. Anything that processes the information in the head will help.

Radio advertisers today need to know about chunking, then they could chunk as they recite numbers. Instead of reading "six, four, one, two," they could just say "sixty-four, twelve." People could easily remember that long enough to get a pencil and write it down, and the announcers could quit their irritating three-time repetition that has become standard procedure. Reading it only once or possibly twice would be sufficient. Children who learn about chunking can chunk in their own heads even if announcers and speakers do not do it for them.

Checklist

Keep a list of literary, history, and Bible passages that your children memorize, and make an effort to review them occasionally.

8 Writing Skills

Learning to write during the early years is not hard if you keep it natural. Think back on your child beginning to talk. At first he spoke just a word now and then. You reinforced by responding with pleasure, perhaps repeating the word yourself to model a good pronunciation. You didn't think, "Oh, now I should start lessons—a word or two each day, then sentences, then . . ." No, you just tuned in to the child's thinking and went along with his pace.

Transfer that procedure to writing. One day the child wants to write his name, so you help by making a model for him to trace or to copy. The teacher in you does not need to think that next you should teach his sister's name or the whole alphabet or any other sequence of learning. Just tune in to his pace. You do not even have to plan review lessons, though you might sneak one in by saying, "We need your name on this box," and the child can proudly use his skill.

Writing mechanics. For several years you need only teach your children "writing mechanics," the skills used for writing but not for speaking. Children already know the grammar. They speak sentences, use plurals and past tense, and numerous grammar items. So do not crowd your curriculum with language lessons that teach those matters. Concentrate, instead, on getting sentences onto paper with correct capitalization, punctuation, and spelling.

Learning letters can at first be piecemeal, not in any particular sequence. Children learn to recite the spelling of their own name. From storybooks they learn that Jesus is the word that begins with *J,* and so on. Once they acquire this meaning of what letters do, you can begin teaching them to write all the letters, not necessarily in alphabetical order, but any letters they need for their own writing. A simple wall chart for reference will help for quite a while until even the Xs and Vs become second nature. The wall chart can show simple printing style, or italic style if you use that. Keep the chart where children can see it while they are writing. Besides children's writing style, teach the extra "book style" of letters *a* and *g.*

Use printing at first. This is easier for many children because it is closer to the letters they read. And in adult life we need to print clearly when filling out forms, making posters or signs, and other uses. Let your children master both printing and cursive. Switching to cursive, connected writing will be easy and take only about three weeks if you wait until children are adept at printing, about third grade for many children. Use a chart for cursive, too.

Once the time is right, you can make models of words for the children to copy—the child's name, family names, and other words. Next, use sentences from a Bible verse or a storybook, or the child's original sentence. This copying technique involves close study of details. If the child misses something, do not start the negative, discouraging practice of marking errors and punishing by requiring a child to copy a missed word five times or any similar procedure. Improvement comes in time with regular writing practice.

Children are overloaded with details at this early stage of writing, so it helps to keep charts in plain sight. They are learning how each letter is formed, in both capitals and lower case. Where and when to use capitals is new. Punctuation and spelling are new. Children used none of those for speaking. They could do sentences and paragraphs when they spoke or dictated to you, but writing, now, involves the new details of *writing mechanics.*

After a child knows the letters and copies easily, you could begin trying dictation, which is a step up from copying. Some ideas are to choose a sentence from a simple storybook or make a sentence about the morning Bible reading: The men went fishing; Jesus healed a sick man; God parted the Red Sea. You can allow various levels of independence with dictation. At first, read and discuss the sentence and word spellings ahead of time or help with spelling as a child writes. Children can work up to writing a sentence from dictation entirely on their own, and later, a short paragraph. They could first copy something for several days and when they know it well write it from dictation. A valuable part of both copy and dictation writing is for the children to compare their writing with the model and try to find any mistakes. Copying and dictation are handy assignments to do when children do not have something of their own they want to write.

Some girls achieve beautiful handwriting early on. For children whose penmanship looks sloppy but they are doing the best they can, wait awhile for their small muscles to develop further. Then select aspects they need to work on. Is a particular letter poorly formed? Look at the chart and talk about closing the top, making it taller, or whatever is needed. Let them copy the letter two or three times, then copy a word containing the letter. In other words, you decide what to teach and then tutor individually. This is more efficient than hoping the needed lesson will turn up in a book somewhere if a child uses the whole book.

Most children need to improve uniformity of slant and height. This feature helps more than anything to impress people that your children are well educated. Try exaggerated rhythm with a strong beat on the downward strokes of *m* and *n,* then *t* and other letters and short words.

Continue writing for the children at times even after they can write for themselves, just as you continue to read to them after they can read. Overlap the two procedures. The mother of a ten-year-old says the girl looks over her shoulder while she types. As she punctuates or capitalizes she explains some of this to the girl, teaching her in small doses. Sometimes the daughter stops her to explain what punctuation she wants, especially unusual ones like parentheses and exclamation points. Some mothers gently change wording as they type to help teach better usage, not so much as to overwhelm a child, but small doses again. Some mothers have the child write the first sentence, and then they write the rest as the child dictates what he wants to say.

One thirteen-year-old boy wrote long original fiction with a lot of conversation. He knew about periods but not about quotation marks. Punctuating dialog looks complex at first glance, but sit beside a child like this and tutor for a few sentences. Show how to handle the commas and quotation marks and other punctuation. Examine how this is done in a book that is handy. Similar on-the-spot teaching works with many writing problems.

One reason homeschoolers like workbooks is that they think they can measure progress each day—at least progress through the book. But real progress in the skills of reading and writing is not that linear. Look back in three months or at the end of a year and you will be encouraged with good progress after using some of the freer, non-book methods. You can save occasional dated samples of writing for this purpose. During elementary years you are likely to be surprised at the improvement. During junior high years progress may seem slower. Because of growth spurt in the brain as well as the rest of the body, we apparently need to allow priority for that growth and not introduce too many new kinds of learning in the early teen years. Keep the children writing real messages for real audiences and let growth occur as it will.

Message and audience. When children can write a little on their own, find real-life reasons for writing. Work on message more than on comma rules. Help children get something in their heads first. Talk about the field trip. Where did you go? What was most interesting to you? Talk about the day's history reading. Where did those people live? Was it long ago? Tell one or two differences in their lives from ours. What important battle or exploration or other event happened? Once the child has the information somewhat clarified in his head you can assign the writing—not a long report, but a few sentences.

You and other family members can learn to be appreciative audiences. Post some pieces on the refrigerator. Let children pull favorite writings out of their folders to show visitors. Some homeschool groups read their writings to each other and find that highly motivating. Letters always have an audience. Besides writing to friends, relatives, missionaries, and soldiers, sometimes write a letter to an editor or to a congressman or other government official. Or write to a book author. Some children enjoy producing a newsletter for family or neighborhood or church. The computer-savvy child may communicate with interest groups online.

Particular forms such as term paper or essay come later. Even paragraph form of topic sentence, supporting sentences, and summing sentence is an artificial schooling creation. Use the looser paragraph definition of several sentences about a single topic. Most important is that children think and have something to say.

Writing to Learn

In the middle grades, and more so in high school, students are ready to give attention to higher aspects of writing. These older students already know the mechanics of writing so well that their mind is not occupied fully with those details. Most punctuation is second nature. Sentences have long been second nature. Paragraphing is not a major problem. Students may just think, "This is a turn in thought so I'd better start a new paragraph." Their mind is freer now to think like advanced students or more like professional writers. At this time, students are not so much learning to write as writing to learn.

Writing *is* learning. This is an important principle to try to understand. To learn, one must process information in the mind, and writing is a powerful way to process information, in other words to think. Thinking and writing are intertwined all the way from the first information gathering and planning, through the writing and rewriting, to evaluating the work and polishing it. This does not happen in neat step sequence, although workbooks often pretend it does, as one professor phrased it.

The hard work of setting down thoughts clearly and orderly for an audience develops the writer's thinking on his topic so that he gains ideas and insights that he did not have while planning for the writing. One mother complained that her son would not outline before he wrote, but she added that he was a good writer. This boy was operating like most professional writers. Jacques Barzun, a former educator and writer, said, "Outlines are useless, fettering, imbecile." Sometimes when you are mixed up and writing in circles, he said, it may help to jot down a list of topics so far covered, and this may help to show where you got off the track. One man says he flunked college speech class because it really was an Outline 101 class. Now he is a popular talk-show host.

Outlining is not the royal road to good writing. Some people may use it sometimes, and that is the best that can be said for it.

In the list of planning components below, number five is a tentative outline. Other important ways to plan are also listed. Acquaintance with these will help older students to better plan their writing. They can use any one or more and use them in any order.

1. Have a main idea for the writing. What topic will it be about?
2. Choose a focus. From what angle or viewpoint will you approach the topic?
3. Gather information. Do you already know enough information or do you need to collect more?
4. Think about the audience. What is their prior knowledge about this topic and their attitude toward it?
5. Decide tentatively about the organization. How will you begin, in what order will you proceed, and what will be your main emphasis? Organizing reading selections by outlines and graphics prepares for this more difficult task of organizing writing.
6. Analyze the medium you are aiming for. Does it carry news, think pieces, entertaining pieces, or other kinds? Is it for college application?

Students who write fairly well can benefit from reading the above list and becoming aware of what writers do in their planning. Most students will benefit if you can emphasize one of the procedures at an appropriate time. You might say, "First you have to explain this to people before you ask them to write to their congressmen" (4 and 5). Or, "You can't just sort of tell about it like a fourth grader. You need a particular focus and reason for being on this topic" (2).

When the writing and several rewrites are finished it should look well organized, focused, and suited to its purpose. The readers (if not writers themselves) will be unaware of the hard and messy work it took to get there. The harder the writer worked the easier it is to read.

Your older students can try some of the thinking and planning skills listed above, using them for occasional writings, but do not turn every assignment into a full-blown, write-like-a-professional task. Help students work to their limit on a few assignments that are worth it. These selected assignments should come from studies of history, current issues, science, or other content of your children's schooling.

Family Methods

It is fairly easy to get some children to write, while others take more effort. Even the math-oriented students who become engineers will have to write good memos and annual reports, so do all you can for their writing. Encourage at the beginning and all along the way. The schooling system of red penciling "errors" is counterproductive. With that system, children try to write something simple and use only words they know how to spell. They do not stretch their writing ability but aim only to avoid errors.

Also counterproductive is to always say "Look it up" instead of answering a spelling or grammar question. Family members should answer each other's questions as much as possible, and when no one knows the answer then somebody tries to look it up. This teaches a lifelong attitude that yes we do want it right and yes we do have to research sometimes to find an answer. Also it avoids the groans against dictionaries that the look-it-up system brings.

An easy procedure is to have everybody sit down and write for a specified time. You or an older child could take dictation from a young child who does not write yet. Children can copy something or write a letter or work on a history assignment. You could work on writing up a mail order. So all ages can write at the same time. Each child decides on his own what to write during writing time. Try this even with a single child.

This astonishingly simple system really works. At first some children may not come up with writing ideas. If one complains, "What shall I write?" you can answer, "Well, write the number words starting with *one* and see how far you can get." This is not an assignment so much as it is saying, "C'mon, get going with something." If the child actually does write the numbers, he is likely to think of something more interesting for the next day. Older children may work on one project for several days.

Be regular with the writing schedule and it will take only a few days to get it working. Elementary children quickly learn to latch on to an event or dream or pet or almost anything that entered their heads the night before and decide that's what they will write about the next day.

An audience for the writing? After the writing time, volunteers may read aloud what they wrote. Or periodically each person could choose a favorite and read it. You could collect the writings and respond to some in writing and others orally, maybe the next day. You could give special attention to some by reading them aloud to the family while Dad is there.

A variation of this free-writing system is to let the children schedule it into their time. Specify a particular desk tray and explain that each child should put a sheet of writing in there each day. It must be in before they eat lunch or go out to play, or whatever will work in your family. This daily system works best with younger children who are not yet into revising and rewriting. Older children may be given a longer period of time than one day.

Again, figure out ways to give attention and to be an audience for the writing they work so hard to do.

Vary the free writing sometimes when you have an idea for a directed writing lesson. One idea is to have the children write a poem, imitating the pattern of a poem your family has enjoyed. Lesson books often begin with seventeen-syllable haiku or with limericks because they are short and follow a simple formula, but it is a more valuable experience to copy the rhythms and rhyme patterns of an English poem. Use the old style poem (that is returning today) with regular rhyming patterns, not free verse. This attention to English rhythms and sounds is good for all writers of prose, not only of poetry. It develops an ear for excellent English. Repeat the poetry writing every once in a while.

You can also insert from time to time a directed lesson that you like from any writing curriculum you happen to have. Most writing curriculums work well with you picking and choosing what looks helpful for your family. That's because writing skills do not grow one after the other in linear fashion. This non-linear feature makes writing hard to measure and grade day by day. But progress occurs anyway. Parents who give up the struggle with daily workbook lessons and encourage real-life writing and children's choice writing look back months later and are delighted not only with the progress but with the happy times they had.

About half of children like keeping journals. Some write prayer journals, listing prayers and their answers. Some keep devotional journals, recording their thoughts on a Bible reading. Some like the old-fashioned diary that relates the day's happenings. Some can keep short-term diaries on a trip or during a camp week. With even non-journal children you might get them to help keep homeschool records. On notebook pages they could list books read, field trips, and assignments and projects completed. A sentence or two about each book or trip will provide good reminders at end-of-year check up.

Essays

Students who learn to say something clearly to an audience can easily fit into any form they wish to. So before the need appears, students should not spend time learning forms such as news reports or term papers and research papers with footnoting. Even at young ages it does not help to practice the paragraph form of topic sentence, development sentences, and concluding sentence. Real-life writing is not that artificial.

But essay form is so entrenched in our schooling system with its testing that it needs special attention. Essays often are taught as a formula of introductory paragraph, three development paragraphs, and concluding paragraph. A good introduction and conclusion are important, and the development in between could vary from a rigid three paragraphs. During elementary years children learn to write shorter pieces about a single subject. By high school we hope they can organize a few paragraphs into an essay. Mastering essays helps students enter college or win scholarships.

Four types of essays. The most common school essay is called *expository.* It informs the readers about a particular topic. It presents information, explains how something works, or tells how to do something. Students can write expository essays on topics from Bible, history, government, or on any content subjects that they are learning.

Another type is the *persuasive* essay. Here the students argue in favor of something such as why homeschooling is better than public schooling, or why the family should visit Redwood National Park on their vacation. They can prepare for this by making a pro and con chart. On the pro side they list good arguments for their position, and on the con side list the best arguments an opponent might make against it—it is too far, too crowded, or another place is a better choice.

The chart serves as an outline, so in this case it is easier to write the introduction first, announcing what the students will argue for. Then clearly explain the pro arguments and answer the con arguments the best way they can. Use as many paragraphs }as needed. Then sum up by stating how they have more or better arguments, perhaps reminding the readers briefly of what they are. The wrap-up should show that they accomplished what they announced in the introduction. SAT tests often ask for a persuasive essay because students can demonstrate their writing skills without having to know a lot of information on an assigned topic.

A third type of essay is the *descriptive.* Some professionals have made their reputation on wonderful descriptions. They open our eyes to moods and meanings that we would miss on our own, much as a good visual artist does. Students might try that, but they should aim first for accuracy and clarity. A profitable thinking exercise is to reverse descriptive writing. That is, when you find a descriptive paragraph then have a student show his understanding by sketching the scene. If you have a writing-hater, try this. Writers, too, can profit. It will help them write a clearer description the next time they need to do one.

A fourth type of essay is the *narrative.* It is a story usually told in first person using the pronoun *I,* but it also can be about somebody else and be told in third person using *he* or *she.* In narrative it is comparatively easy to write an orderly progression of thoughts. To succeed as an essay, the narrative must make a point that is helpful to the reader. For instance, the story might tell of meeting with a mountain lion, but the writer remembered not to turn and run. He backed off slowly, talking loudly and firmly to the lion, not looking him in the eyes, and spreading out his arms and coat to look big. Details of the story make interesting reading, and the lesson about how to handle the situation will be helpful to the readers—if they ever meet a mountain lion.

Personal narratives of the getting-to-know-you type are often found on college applications. They ask what are your dreams and ambitions, what one policy would you implement if you were president for a day, or if you wrote a memoir of your life through high school what would you choose for a title and why. Students can practice writing about themselves and their experiences so they feel ready for questions like these.

Essays for tests. In test situations, students do not get to rewrite and edit and fix up the essay. They have to show what they can do on the spot and turn in the first draft.

Scorers of SAT essays are usually high school or college English teachers. They rate on a scale of 6 to 0. Score 6 is outstanding, 5 effective, and 4 competent in these traits: reasoning and thinking, organization and focus, variety of sentence structure, appropriate vocabulary, and grammar and mechanics. Score 3 is inadequate, 2 seriously limited, and 1 fundamentally lacking in those same traits. An essay not written on the assigned topic receives a 0.

Scorers are told to remember that they are scoring the writing and not the accuracy of the information. One professor found that longer essays tend to score higher regardless of the quality. Knowing this, students should not stall and lose time during a test if they are not sure about facts. They should keep writing good sentences and keep their arguments flowing, even if not entirely accurate.

Rewriting. Students at the essay level, particularly high school students, can work on rewriting after the first draft. James A. Michener, a Pulitzer Prize novelist, wrote, "I have never been able to write anything that could stand in the first draft." With all

Michener's experience you might think that he learned to write something correctly and well the first time. But he wrote first drafts and revisions even of his personal letters that had an audience of one.

Students should begin rewriting by tackling the biggest matters. Does the writing say what they want to say in an orderly manner? Juggle things around until it does. Cut parts that get off the track. Be brutal with cuts needed in the precious writing.

They can try to be one of their future readers. Does a statement need an illustration to help readers understand better? Think of one and add it. Does a section sound muddy? Rewrite it. Are some parts not really on the mark for the message, but maybe good thoughts that they managed to sneak in? Delete them. Use more cutting than pasting, according to some authors. Are they really trying to say two things, and that leads to mix-ups? Separate them. Write down all illustrations and arguments for one message and then move on to the second message. Or save it for another essay. If an idea up here fits better with something down there, circle it and draw a pencil line down to where it belongs.

Does the opening properly introduce the message? Does the closing satisfy? Closings often circle back to the opening and say in effect, "See, I told you what I promised to tell you at the beginning." When the papers are good and messy, make the changes on computer, print a new copy, and repeat the whole process as many times as needed until the writing is well organized. Help as you can with ideas for improving the writing.

When the essay seems quite orderly, give attention to the smaller matters of rewording parts for more clarity and better style of English. Students should use everything they know about good writing for this step. Refer to any writing curriculum or writing style books you have for tips such as eliminating wordiness, enlivening the verbs, and changing passive sentences to active.

After organizing and after clarifying, you arrive at last at the editing and proofing step. From teaching your children through the lower grades, you may have concluded that this is the important, first, or only step to take. But for your advanced writers this is the last step. Students should check reference books for any word that may be misspelled or any wording that may be grammatically incorrect.

Learning to write is a lifelong endeavor—for homeschool students and for their parents, who strengthen society with their own writings. All must work hard at rewriting. Robert Louis Stevenson said, "When I say writing, O, believe me, it is rewriting I have chiefly in mind." Other writers echo that statement, saying that there is no good writing, only good rewriting.

Checklist

This list is a reminder of some of the ideas mentioned in this chapter. You could jot down if you have already tried an item or are now trying it or wish to try it later with your children.

1. Wall or desk chart of letters   _____
2. Audiences for children's writing   _____
3. English poem structures   _____
4. Techniques in the planning list   _____
5. All-family writing time   _____

9 Grammar after Writing

The homeschool community is being oversold on grammar. The following information can help you avoid being oversold. First, we see how grammar originated and developed, and how educators came to misuse it. Then we look at the solution, which is to delay teaching grammar through the elementary years, and show some of the reasons for delaying. This can simplify your homeschooling life, help you spend less on curriculum, and help you teach writing more easily. Your children will profit from a stronger writing foundation, and in the end they will turn out to be better writers, not burned out on grammar along the way.

How Did Grammar Come to Us?

Here is a bit of history of how grammar came to us. A Greek named Dionysus Thrax developed the "science" of grammar. It was not used to help with teaching or to help children grasp their language. Instead, it was an advanced science of analyzing the words of language. Homer and other poets, playwrights, and classic philosophers had already written, without benefit of Thrax's grammar.

Romans adopted the Greek model, but it was not a good fit for their language. For instance, Greek had articles (a, an, the), and Latin did not. The Romans managed by listing demonstrative pronouns (this, that) instead. They adapted on other points, too. Once they made rules based on the Greek, they grew tyrannical about the way people *should* write, rather than teaching the way good writers *do* write.

Englishmen imported Latin and repeated that process. In America's early days those who could afford it attended Latin grammar schools where they obtained a true Latin education, studying ancient writers in their original Latin language. When Latin grammar schools began to give way to English grammar schools, we wanted English grammar books. As the Romans had done, we used our predecessor for a model; the textbook writers patterned English grammar after Latin grammar. This, again, was a poor fit. For instance, Latin verb infinitives were single words, while English infinitives were two words: *to run, to close, to split,* etc. So grammarians proclaimed that we should not "split" infinitives. Romans could not split their one-word infinitives, so we should not split ours, even though ours are two words and even though sentences sometimes are stronger with a word between the two.

Prepositions differed also. In Latin they are prefixes attached to their words. The very word means *pre-position*. We inherit many of those Latin prepositions: *in*dent, *trans*port, *sub*marine. It is impossible to end a sentence with Latin prepositions, and thus arose the myth that we should not do so in English either. Everybody has heard Winston Churchill's comment: "This is the kind of English up with which I will not put." Actually, that was diluted for American ears. He originally wrote a more colorful

British idiom in the margin of a speechwriter's proposal: "This is the kind of bloody nonsense up with which I will not put."

Another problem: What should the grammar books say about cases? Latin had nominative, dative, accusative, and more. In English we do not have all these. We show possessive case by adding apostrophe *s,* but do not otherwise change word forms of verbs, nouns, or their modifiers. Only a few pronouns change word forms for case (I, me, my; he, him, his). Neither do our verbs have a future tense. We express future *time* in various ways, but not by changing the verb *tense.* We say "I will go" or "I plan to go," but the word *go* remains the same form. It has no form for future tense. Grammar books became filled, anyway, with complex teaching similar to Latin grammar books.

In these many ways, English grammarians tried to force English into the Latin mold. Some grammarians and educators in recent decades modified their teachings to fit English better, and a backlash developed. People objected that they were dumbing down English teaching. This backlash persisted and even grew in the homeschool movement. Homeschoolers feel pressured to outdo public schools, and heavy grammar teaching is sold as one way to accomplish that.

What Does Grammar Do for Writing?

No research anywhere shows that learning grammar helps students become better writers. There is no correlation between knowledge of grammar and ability to write well. This topic has been researched for practically a century because there has always been high interest in the question. We researched not only the Latin style grammars but also newer ones called generative, transactional, and others. We researched this method and that method with this content and that content, and all the research was negative. An engineer says he loved diagramming sentences. The logic challenged his engineering mind, but the method of diagramming was included in the grammar research and also shown to have no effect on improving children's writing.

Some adults say that they finally understood grammar when they took Latin. They never say that it helped them to write better, only that they then could see a reason for the cases and other features the English teacher had tried to teach them. Of course. That's because the grammar fits Latin and they finally studied the Latin to go with it. Even the Latin study does not improve children's writing.

So we should know better. But research does not drive education. Often money does. If people will buy grammar textbooks, publishers will publish them regardless of what research says.

Native speakers of English automatically learn its grammar. By age four or five, children know considerable grammar without us specifically teaching it to them. You may correct them if they say "I knowed," and they learn to say "I knew." But their first use—I knowed—follows the rule of forming past tense by adding the *d* sound, so even the mistake shows that the child uses that grammar rule. By school age, children also use interrogative, declarative, and exclamatory sentences. They use present and past tense of verbs, and express future time. They use nouns with singular and plural forms and with modifiers, pronouns with three cases (I, me, my), prepositions, conjunctions, and other function words.

School age children continue this natural learning of grammar, and by age ten they use the level of grammar that speakers around them use. Since children speak the plural *s* and the past tense *ed,* you need not teach abstract grammar about number and tense. Just help them spell those endings. They already speak possessive case (Henry's ball) so just show them that we write it with apostrophe *s.* Save the grammar for sometime in their teen years.

Then they will become educated about it, but will not have been burned out on it, and they may actually enjoy it at that time.

Prescription or Description?

Latin-oriented grammar tends to consist of rules that *prescribe* how to write rather than *describing* the forms used by the best writers. Does Latin have a perfect grammar worthy of being prescribed for English? Many people think so. They come to that opinion because editors have "fixed" Latin over the years. The library of Latin books that we inherit fills only about one wall of one room. When a book came up for reprint, the proofreaders would change its usages to make each conform to some rule or other. It is like passing a law and making it retroactive. Publishers decided on these changes, and in time all the grammar became consistent. We now have the "perfect" language. It is dead and cannot fight back. English is living; it continues to fight. The prescription method acts as if English language is dead already. Its grammatical rules are supposed to be set in stone. We must teach the formulas and follow them. Don't think for yourself; just follow the prescription that the doctor ordered.

If you believe in the descriptive system instead of the prescriptive, you will immerse your children in good reading. They will write often. In teen years they will learn some grammar, but by that time they will find that they conform to most of it already. It did not help them become good writers, but being good writers helped them understand grammar. A high school girl reading a grammar book for the first time suddenly exclaimed, "Mom, this is interesting!"

The Ear Approach

Who or whom. Since children automatically learn the grammar of the people around them, their ear can guide on most matters, even difficult ones like the who-whom problem. We all remember from high school that *who* is nominative case and *whom* is objective. But we all constantly meet puzzles, especially in questions: "Whom do you admire the most?" Change it to a statement and substitute *he* or *him*: "You admire *him*." This shows that you need object form. Fortunately, you need to puzzle about nominative or objective forms only with pronouns. That's one advantage English has over Latin.

With questions, we have a tendency to treat *who* like the interrogative words *when, where,* and *why*. Thus in speech people may say "Who do you admire?" but in writing they are more formal and write "Whom do you admire?"

Sometimes the pronoun belongs to a clause within a sentence: "Michael, *whom* everyone called Shorty . . . " or "Michael, *who* is called Shorty . . . " Again, the ear can help. We would say "Everyone called *him* Shorty" and "*He* is called Shorty." *Him,* then, indicates that *whom* belongs in the first clause, and *he* indicates that *who* belongs in the second clause.

Students can wrestle with these grammar gymnastics late in their schooling or in their writing life, but these certainly are not the route to learning how to write. Use the ear approach instead, taking advantage of the grammar children already know in their speaking.

Word order. In English, we understand by the order of the words, not by inflected word forms as in Latin. One word-order pattern is that we tend to use *me* at the end of a sentence just because it is at the end. "Who's there?" "It's me." Only the high school English teacher or her *A* student is likely to answer "It is I." They inherited the Latin grammar emphasis on cases, which teaches that following the *is* verb, the pronoun *I* is the same case as the subject *it*. They both should be nominative per Latin grammar. Without that Latin grammar teaching, the *me* ending would probably have won out. For now, we live with conflict between the two systems—word-order and case. The song says, "It's a me, O Lord, standing in the need of prayer." On the other hand, the Little Red Hen, the Cat, the Duck, and others all say "Not I" until it comes time to eat the bread. A new book imitating the story says "Not me."

We would be better off in the *me* problem if word-order had won out. That would rescue people from saying even in sermons and radio programs that "the team joined Julie and I" or "the promises are for you and I." These speakers are trying to please their English teacher, but they miss. This usage is wrong by both the Latin-grammar system and the English word-order system. Latin calls for *me* in object position, and word-order English calls for *me* in end position. It is easy to teach your children what to write in sentences about two people. Forget all the grammar explanations and use the ear again. Tell them to leave off the extra person in the sentence and see which sounds right, *I* or *me*.

Grammar Last

After learning to speak and then learning to write, students can begin to handle a formal study of grammar. Some verbally oriented students or those who understand abstractions will take to this more readily than others. Those who take up writing full- or part-time are likely to make this a lifelong study. We do them a favor by not boring them or burning them out on grammar while they are young. The schooling world and the advertising world have convinced many people that to teach language you *must* teach grammar, and you must begin early as though that is the route to good writing and speaking. But the real route is to *use* the language first, immerse children in the language, and then teach its grammar.

This delay of grammar and minimizing of grammar is not at all to minimize English teaching. Quite the opposite. If your children are not burdened with difficult and ineffective grammar, then they have more time for learning that counts.

Grammar materials. Some homeschool suppliers offer books planned for the grammar-later approach. You can even find a one-book format to use instead of the grade-by-grade format. That is the best of all. A one-book grammar will earn a place alongside your dictionary on a bookshelf. Students can study parts of it at times and use it for reference at other times. Later the book can go to college with them, if that is where they are headed, and can go with them into adult life. That is book money well spent. Better yet, it is time well spent.

These one-book grammars may say they are for grades seven to twelve or that they fit ages twelve and up. That should not mean they have lessons spread out year by year. Hopefully it means that the grammar information is there in organized form and you can use it when and where you like in the upper grades. When you obtain one of these grammar books, you can look it over, read parts, and see what is there. Then you can better decide what parts to use for a lesson on grammar now and then. You might choose something you want to learn alongside your children. That is a major perk of being a teacher; you get to relearn what you have forgotten since your own school days.

You can see some of the grammar hype by perusing advertisements and catalog blurbs. There are numerous grade-by-grade books, some starting at grade one and others starting at grade three. You can skip the graded books altogether. One problem with these, especially the workbooks, is that they have no afterlife. Who goes to their pile of worn workbooks when they want to look up some information? Another problem with fill-in-the-blank assignments is that they are not a very effective learning method.

Also, the early use of workbooks burns children out on workbooks. This effect shows up by third grade.

Ads often stress that materials focus on rules. This gives a clue that a product uses the prescriptive approach. Practice and drill materials are prescriptive, oriented to following formulas and rules. Their rules most likely are geared to the Latin-style grammar rather than to English. Ads seem never to address the subject of how Latin-oriented the product is, but you can often tell by using this "rule" clue. Some ads reveal the current confusion about what grammar is, lumping it together with writing mechanics or even reducing it totally to mere mechanics, as an ad that says their books teach "grammar mechanics." Other ads blow up grammar to mean total language learning, such as changing the traditional 3Rs into "reading, *grammar,* and arithmetic."

Not only the ads, but reviews, too, can lead down the grammar path. An example is a curriculum review that described an integrated curriculum and "warned" that it contained little grammar, so you would have to add grammar to it. Containing little grammar should be a plus for that curriculum, not a flaw.

Besides texts, there are workbooks, worksheets, CD-ROMs, and games. You can skip most of these grammar materials, too. Products that advertise they are amusing and fun imply that grammar is intrinsically dull. That follows from the practice of beginning grammar at young ages before children can understand abstractions, and from boring them with it every grade through school. When a subject engages the mind it involves the learners, and you do not need games and glitz to attract them to it. By teen years grammar can be interesting in itself, or at least understandable.

We need a major turn-around in the grammar and writing fields, and in homeschooling that can happen family by family. One mother listened to this advice and turned 180 degrees while her daughter was in third grade. She wrote, "We had a wonderful year! I was able to let go of the curriculum I had purchased and as a result, we became very relaxed in our schooling. Her reading and writing improved a lot, with no interference from me. . . . I'm at peace with both." Letting go of the textbook pressure can help you, also, to simplify your teaching of English. Begin writing mechanics as soon as children write, and teach correct usage anytime you hear something incorrect. But save formal grammar for later years. This arrangement is simple and powerful.

10 Informal Beginnings

Did you ever notice that homeschool moms and their children play School, while good teachers at school play Home? In many cases that is exactly what happens. And sometimes the moms' picture of what School should be is rather grim.

Take, for instance, the mother of a three-year-old who ran herself ragged with field trips to the bakery, the post office, and local historic sights, and with trying to find reading related to the trips so they could qualify as School units. She made sack lunches for the busy, rushed days.

A good preschool teacher, meanwhile, was playing Home the best she could with a large class of children. They gathered round and helped measure and pour ingredients into a bowl. They took turns stirring. They each got a piece of dough to shape into a biscuit. They cleaned flour off their hands and waited impatiently for the biscuits to bake in another part of the building, since the classroom was not homelike enough to have an oven. At last they sat down to spread butter and jelly and enjoy eating a biscuit.

They remembered flour and dough—first-hand experience—not at all like the bewildering big bakery the homeschooler visited. If they ever did visit a bakery later, they would have a little background to understand better what was going on.

Listen to this preschool mom. "I had a hard time sticking with it every day and sometimes took the day off. Now I'm behind and I have to teach five days a week through the end of the school year to complete the curriculum. The first week back after Christmas was *torture* for both of us. I tried my best to be upbeat, positive, and fun. My son tried his best to be grouchy, whiney, and impossible. By Wednesday I was convinced I should send him to school after preschool. But by Friday I felt selfish and decided I'd better keep this up at least through kindergarten. Maybe our curriculum now is too sit-down, boring, and workbook-based, though I don't think it is too hard for him. For kindergarten I need a more fun, hands-on curriculum that still has high academic standards."

Somebody, please tell these mothers to relax and enjoy their young children. If you know either kind—the workbook slave or the see-everything mom—go rescue her. These moms need to know that what the children need most is their natural, loving, peaceful home environment. They learn more this way than with School.

Natural Learning

Did you teach your child to walk? Most families, particularly with their first child, enjoy helping along those early steps. They hold the child's hands to steady him. They applaud and encourage each sign of improvement. Then one memorable day he takes some steps entirely on his own. Success!

But wait. Researchers say that child would have walked just as soon without all the help. His walking depended on maturation and not on teaching.

This same principle applies with most early learning. All that babbling in the crib is phonics practice. The baby tries out all the sounds he can make. After practice he becomes skilled enough that he can select the sounds he needs to say dada or mama or other words he hears. The child is so good at phonics sounds that up to about age seven he could learn to speak in any language. But his family teaches him one or two languages and he loses his ability to make sounds that he does not use in those languages. (If you can keep alive this ability for all sounds, then the child will be a better speaker of any language he later learns.)

The two-year-old learns about eight new words per day without any vocabulary lessons. She puts together two-word sentences at first, then on up to six-word sentences by age three without any grammar lessons.

Scribbling, too, is self-learning. Children learn the motor skills of pushing a crayon in any and all directions. More importantly, they learn mentally what writing is. Jon brought a scribbled paper to his mother and asked, "What does this say?" She couldn't say, "It doesn't say anything, Honey. You have to learn how to write." So she took the paper and began to read, "For God so loved the world that he gave his only begotten son . . . Oops, it's not finished." Jon eagerly scribbled some more to finish the verse. They played this game for a couple of days and then Jon moved on to other learning.

Young children, like Jon, are always learning. It would be hard to stop them, but we seem to work at it by instituting formal teaching far too early. American day-care centers and preschools did not originate from any need of children to be removed from their homes and taught "academics." They mostly originated during

World War II when millions of men went off to war and millions of women went off to factories. The preschools filled a childcare need, not an academic need. But once the teachers' union gained this slice of the economy, they would not let go.

Publishers, too, gain from having more students to sell books for. Consumable workbooks were invented about 1930 and used at first in elementary grades, at least in school districts that could afford them. As kindergartens spread and preschools spread, publishers could sell more and more workbooks, and somehow we have come to believe they are necessary. The harried mom who said the work was not too hard for her son was really saying that he knows all that stuff, so why can't he do it in a book. You will often find that your children know the stuff, even up to first and second grade arithmetic books. Try looking at what a page teaches, and then try the same problems in real life. Can the child put two more plates on the table? How many plates are now on the table? If they already know the stuff, they do not need the books, and if they don't know, it is better to teach with plates and other real objects than with books.

Some of the whining and grouchiness the children show could be that close bookwork is hard on their eyes at young ages. They don't understand that and can't explain. They just resist in whatever ways they can. Also hand-dominance (left or right) is not settled yet at preschool ages, and fine motor skills are usually not developed for exacting bookwork.

If preschool is too early for formal academics, then what about kindergarten? Is that the time to start? The answer again is no. Modern kindergartens started in Italy under Maria Montessori and in Germany under Friedrich Froebel. Both worked with poor and disadvantaged children of working mothers to try to prepare them for school. They provided experiences that middle-class families normally provide. Middle-class families talk with their children more, read to them, and let them handle and play with things. In general they provide a good learning environment even if they are not specifically trying to.

Our society now is obsessed with academic teaching more and more, earlier and earlier. It is fine for children to learn in the kitchen or laundry room with Mom, or in the garage with Dad, or at play with siblings. But the race to memorize phonics or number "facts" earlier and earlier is no help for children's later academic achievement. It succeeds, instead, in wasting time that could be spent more profitably on other pursuits.

Sometimes a younger child wants to "do school" because siblings are doing school. In such cases, you can let the child have a colorful workbook to use his way. He plays with it, using either hand he happens to use; he does not have to be neat or correct; and he stops when he tires of it. Short periods like that should be safe enough for the eyes.

An oft-quoted myth is that children by age five learn half of all they will ever learn. The source of this myth is some complex research by Jerome Bruner in which he compared scores from IQ tests across ages and concluded as best he could from the different kinds of tests that children's mental ability is half developed at age five. (It completes in late teens.) He did not say that children at age five have finished half their learning. The myth spreaders misinterpret the information to mean that young, still-developing children have learned half of what a fifty-year-old professor knows. That looks absurd on the face of it, but the myth perpetuates anyway. This pressures parents to pressure their children with formal education at young ages.

Homeschoolers have opportunity for a fresh, commonsense approach to early childhood learning. We need not follow the misguided earlier-is-better approach of the schooling industry.

The Immersion Method

Educators know immersion as an effective method. They try to use it in foreign languages or in English as a second language classes but are unable to use the method much elsewhere. At home it is easy—and natural.

The immersion method is exactly what it sounds like. You immerse children in a quiet family lifestyle, a non-drug-abuse society, the English language, or whatever. With your preschoolers at home you use this method all the time. That is one reason that homeschooling is so powerful

One immersion teaching is **nutrition**. You do this meal-by-meal and snack-by-snack. Your family sits down to enjoy good food together. Occasionally you may talk about including protein, minimizing sugar, or some new discovery you just read. All this promotes a healthy-eating lifestyle, the outcome that curriculum plans hope to achieve.

Compare your home teaching with a group of kindergartners listening to a teacher explain about proteins and carbohydrates. She may use visuals and activities and other supposedly good teaching methods. She may have a snack time or even a mealtime to use while trying to interact with at least some of the children; but she cannot come close to the immersion system you use.

Add exercise, sleep habits, cleanliness, cheerful mental outlook, and any other aspects of a **healthy lifestyle** you wish. Your immersion teaching gets directly to the desired outcome. The outcome is not tacked on at the end of a lesson plan and called *application.*

Another topic the preschools like to handle is **safety**. Your young children may carry scissors or pencils with the points upward. Explain what could happen if they stumbled and fell onto the sharp object. Use numerous reminders if necessary. You probably use the same procedure concerning radios or other electric items near the bathtub and the safe handling of any tools you allow the children to use. When you teach about hot items, cars, poison, and of course guns, these situations are right where the children live—the stove or iron or traffic in their own environment. Though our adult responsibility is to keep such dangers away from children as much as possible, an even greater responsibility is to teach safety attitudes they can carry through life. At times your family could have a one- or two-lesson unit, such as what to do in case of fire.

A topic taught in all kindergartens and many preschools is **community helpers**. This can include many sub-topics beginning with firemen and policemen, and on to church, medical, postal, merchant, road and construction workers. The curriculum idea is that young children first learn about their own home and family, then about their community, and then the larger world—a plan that radiates outward. This plan got scrambled a bit with the advent of television. Young children can watch world scenes before they know much about their own community. That does not mean, though, that they understand the world scenes.

You do community immersion teaching unavoidably when your children go with you on errands. With a little thought you can stretch this. Notice and talk about a police car or ambulance when you see one. Figure out what the road crews are doing. Stop and examine a construction project. You probably already do these kinds of activities, because you already have the homeschooling mind-set.

Compare, again, with school. In classrooms children play Store so they can learn what clerks and customers do, or they play Post Office to learn about stamps and sending mail. All the while, your children are doing the real thing. Of course they also enjoy playing Post Office or Policeman or Doctor. They do a little immersing of their own.

You teach numerous preschool and kindergarten topics by this immersion method. In all of them you expand a child's **vocabulary**—meaningfully, in context. You start in the context and use words that relate to it, while "vocabulary lessons" do the reverse. They start with a word and pull in some context to help teach it. Between the ages of two and six, children learn almost 3000 words per year. You cannot do that well in elementary grades with vocabulary lessons. Let the natural immersion system of language learning work in the early years and continue it through the school years, too.

Children, and all of us, have several levels of vocabulary use. One level is understanding certain words when someone else uses them, but not using them ourselves. A middle level is originally learning to use the words, as when we talk about something new in a book. A higher level is familiarity so that we freely use the words. To move up to the free-use level your children must meet a word about fourteen times or more. That is one reason that the isolated vocabulary lessons do not work well. Your home immersion method is more powerful.

Conversing is teaching. One family decided they would homeschool in the fall. The mother remarked that they enjoyed their next auto trip more than ever. They had not officially started to homeschool yet, but their mind-set was new. On this trip they talked with the children instead of just telling them to be quiet and sit down. You naturally talk with your children as you shop together, make popcorn together, say good night at bedtime, and so forth. Good teachers would love to provide such an environment for each child, but that is impossible in a classroom. Remember that you have better. Avoid importing the school system into your home.

Children's best language learning comes from interaction with people, particularly with parents. This builds the foundation for all language—reading, writing, grammar, speaking, listening, vocabulary, spelling, thinking—even phonics, since phonics begins with hearing and saying the sounds correctly. Sometimes you might specifically work at this, as, for instance, making sure a child pronounces the first *r* in library and February, the *c* in picture, and the *g* in recognize. Other times this learning continues, anyway, without you thinking about it.

It requires only a little thought or awareness to take advantage of life opportunities as they arise in your family. Children learn more from real life and home than from the game of School.

Art

Manipulative stage. Paints, crayons, and clay all require practice just like the babbling in the crib. Push and pull and swirl and poke. What all can a child do with the medium he has? Someday he might look at a circle he made and see it as a person. He drew it first and named it afterward. Later he becomes able to announce beforehand that he will draw a person. This works both with clay and with drawing. Three phases of learning to manipulate materials are:

1. The child explores, trying out all kinds of movements
2. The child recognizes some forms he made and names them
3. The child announces or plans beforehand what he will make

Through all that manipulative stage we can enjoy trying to understand the children's thinking. What is going on in their minds? How are they growing? We should forget our adult obsession with the end products, with making something that we recognize.

Representative stage. After children can plan what they are going to make, they move gradually into the representative stage. This is about ages four and five and continuing into primary ages for most children. Through all this time we still must focus on children's mental development rather than hand development. As therapists tell paralysis victims: The talent is in your head not your hand. So they learn to paint with the brush in their mouth.

For children, we can teach them to observe and get things into their heads. That is different from showing them how to draw a house, a tree, a boy. On their own, children gradually reach out and try drawing more and more objects. But after some lessons on how to draw specific objects, they regress in their creativity and draw only what they have been taught to draw. Some regress even further and go back to the manipulative stage of randomly scribbling with the paints or whatever materials they are given.

A large research of several hundred children showed this regression. Researchers watched for two years as the children creatively advanced in their drawing skills. Then half the children received ten lessons on drawing something restrictively just the way the teacher told them to. They copied or traced drawings, followed teacher instructions line by line, or colored ready-made drawings. After the ten lessons all children, about six years old by then, took a field trip to a fire station. Back at school, they could make drawings of anything they wanted to from their trip. The "creative" children tried to depict a fire truck or something that impressed them on the trip, some more readily and more successfully than others. Children with the "restrictive" lessons drew flowers, trees, and other items that they had been taught in their ten lessons.

Overwhelming evidence is on the side of letting young children develop their art awareness naturally. Enjoy watching them move through the manipulative stage with no pushing from you. Then in the representative stage, watch and appreciate how they make a man or other object. Sometimes they mix the manipulative phase with this representative phase. That is, they may announce "I'll make me" and proceed to draw a circle for the face, put two eyes on it, and maybe other parts. Then they may put two ears on top and call it a rabbit, then add more lines and forget about what it is. It is "pretty" that way, or funny or whatever the child may wish to call it.

Through all these manipulations the child's mind is busy working and growing. We should not interfere. All those statistics you read about short attention span come from researches where the child is supposed to follow a teacher-imposed task. If you tell a child to draw a particular object or to color within the lines in a coloring book, and if you insist he stay with the task, that is when his attention span is likely to be short. If you allow his mind to work in its own stage of development, the span can be surprisingly long. Moreover, this allows his mind and his motor skills to develop better.

After children can announce and draw objects, they begin to combine two or more objects in a "picture." Sizes often depend on how important an object is. For instance, mother may be larger than the house. Later, a "baseline" appears. This is the ground or the floor upon which to place objects. It is not a horizon. Still later a "skyline" may appear, and there will be space between it and the baseline.

Because of these and other unique features, children's art has become a genre of its own to appreciate and enjoy. Frame a piece and hang it prominently. Sometimes a child may name a picture and you can label it and place it in a folder to save. You could date it, too, and thus form a record of his art development. The purpose of this is simply to enjoy the art, not to prove to anybody that your school is showing progress. Don't spoil all this fun by letting society pressure you into the earlier-is-better mode of thinking. Don't let booksellers pressure you into buying art curriculum at young ages. And don't let friends convince you that your child needs pictures to color within the lines.

Music

One young mother carried her infant to adult church each Sunday until the music was finished. Then she took him to the nursery. An Eskimo mother taught her friends that it was important to sing to their unborn children. Through the toddler age even the most unmusical of parents know enough to help their children learn music. If you can sing "Happy Birthday," you know enough music to teach two- and three-year-olds—at home and at church too. Most preschoolers do not carry a tune yet. They try to follow the singing, usually dragging along behind. So your single voice works best for this. Piano accompaniment adds clutter, and recorded accompaniment adds even more clutter. A trained adult voice has overtones above the main pitch. This gives a rich quality but makes it more difficult for young children to match the pitch. So all you who think you do not sing well, your voice—not too rich, not too high—is just what preschoolers need as they learn to sing.

Three major aspects of music are rhythm, melody, and harmony. Preschoolers first learn rhythm. Children love to clap and march, and preschool teachers concentrate on these rhythm aspects of music. Rhythm instruments add variety—a pair of sticks to tap together, a shaker of beans in a small plastic bottle. Any number of household items make good instruments. Tap a stick onto a pan lid for a beautiful "cymbal" tone. Try them out. Stainless steel seems to work best.

Through all the rhythm stage of teaching, your children should continue to hear music at church, in family singing, or anywhere. Both rhythm and melody skills continue to develop through the kindergarten years. When children enter first grade about half of them can carry a tune, so school music programs begin then to try to teach every child to match tones and sing the melody. At fourth grade they begin learning harmony. Your kindergarten children may or may not be able to sing on tune. Just keep exposing them to music as much as convenient. They will develop their ability.

Memorizing

Memorizing Scripture is a most valuable activity for preschoolers and kindergartners. At home you can reinforce the verses your children learn in Sunday school and elsewhere. Review often so your children overlearn them for longtime retention rather than using the quote-and-forget method.

Kindergartners can learn longer Bible passages by the whole method as described in the study skills chapter. Besides Bible, teach a table grace and bedtime prayer. Teach your home phone number and parents' adult names. If your child is lost in a mall, you want her to know more than that her mother's name is *Mommy*. Teach your street address also. What if your child wanders a block or two from home and somebody asks, "Where do you live?" What will she answer?

Memorize days of the week and, later, months of the year—gradually, not all at once. Begin by simply using the names in conversation: Tomorrow is Sunday so we need to get our church clothes ready. Memorize poems. Recall your own childhood rhymes: Jack and Jill went up the hill; Thirty days hath September; Bye, baby bunting, Daddy's gone a-hunting. The rhymes and rhythms of these poems help prepare children for phonics and other language learning later on.

Memorizing the Bible and other literature develops a good ear for language and its grammar. This is a satisfying activity; do not push it to be hard work. It may be the most valuable language activity young children do. Make a checklist of items your child has memorized so you can use it occasionally for review. Below is a list of memory items mentioned in this section. Add other Scriptures or poems that your child memorizes.

Checklist of Memory Passages

Bible passages   ____

_____

_____

Table grace   ____
Bedtime prayer   ____
Phone, address, family names   ____
Days of the week   ____
Months of the year   ____
Poems   ____

_____

_____

Pre-Reading

Teaching phonics and reading is *not* of first importance for preschoolers and kindergartners as our earlier-is-better society seems to think. Reading *to* children is important, though. Stories for young children have patterns and sequence. These features build thinking skills while also building vocabulary and ear for the phonics sounds and grammar of the language.

If a child asks about a word or a letter, go ahead and answer her. But that in itself does not mean she is ready to begin a formal reading program. One five-year-old said, "I want to learn to read." So her mother taught her three consonant sounds and short *a* sound from a tiny beginning reading book. The girl then could read the book. She carried it around and read it to everybody she met. The next day her mother called her for the next lesson, and she said, "I don't want reading lessons. I just want to read this book." Allow time for these early learnings to digest and grow into fuller understanding.

Some children will begin learning to read at kindergarten age or occasionally younger, but there is nothing to gain, in fact a lot to lose, by trying to push all children into this schedule. Buying the expensive phonics kits assumes you plan to spend years drilling and playing its games and trying to get your money's worth. Free play in the back yard does more for developing thinking skills and preparing for reading.

In one research, three kindergartens were drilled with a typical kindergarten phonics system. Three other kindergartens spent that time learning science with home-like experiences as might happen in a kitchen. They learned liquid, solid, freeze, boil, temperature, sweet, sour, and numerous words and ideas. The six kindergartens were followed through third grade and the phonics children tested lower in reading than the science children. The early start in phonics did not produce better readers, but much advertising hype today tries to make us think so.

The science kindergartens in this research learned their phonics with less time and less effort at a later, more appropriate, age. Instead of a year of drill on phonics, they had time to learn more about their world and thereby to increase their vocabulary and thinking skills. So they had more in their heads to bring to reading, and this made them better readers. Early drill on phonics did not do it; normal learning and development did.

Workbooks in general, on phonics or any topic, retard children's learning as shown in another large research. The researchers followed thousands of children from kindergarten through third grade. Those who started workbooks in kindergarten were burned out on them by third grade, but the others could enjoy learning from them. Another problem is that close attention to books damages eye development. Also, fine motor development may not be ready, and hand dominance not yet settled. This last is a particular problem for children who were born to be left-handed; if they are forced to use their right hand it leads to future neurological learning difficulties.

It is too early to worry if your children are not beginning to read yet. Let them be children. Enjoy them and love them. Let them develop naturally. Resist the temptation of showing that your child can already read while only in kindergarten.

A mother announced, "My daughter finished her kindergarten curriculum in two months." The girl had finished the workbook, and the publishers had said that was the kindergarten book, didn't they? What a narrow view of curriculum! Let your preschoolers and kindergartners learn from the wide world of life.

In your Christian homeschool, you are concerned with spiritual matters above all else. These spiritual tasks or understandings are seldom included in education lists for young children unless someone wants to sound inclusive of body, mind, and spirit. Below is a list of only the spiritual development tasks because these are not in other lists you might use. The tasks are listed in the order of growth. For instance, the first item—experiencing love—is a prerequisite to a young child becoming aware of the loving God. Each task here leads to the next and all lead up to receiving Jesus as Savior, which often happens around age five in Christian homes.

Spiritual Development Tasks[1]

1. Experiencing love, security, discipline, joy, and worship
2. Beginning to develop awareness and concepts of God, Jesus, and other basic Christian realities
3. Developing attitudes toward God, Jesus, church, self, Bible
4. Beginning to develop concepts of right and wrong
5. Experiencing and acknowledging Jesus Christ as Savior and Lord

11 Curriculum Materials

Curriculum materials are less important than we tend to think. They do not make or break your homeschool—unless you try to use too much. That might break a few things. This chapter paints a big picture of publishers and their various curriculum formats, and it explains how we reached this point of market saturation. It offers guidance in what kinds of curriculum to buy and, more importantly, what *not* to buy. The Bible, of course, is your main textbook, and that is discussed in chapter 1. This chapter includes other books and materials.

The word *curriculum* here is used in its narrow sense to refer not to the full learning environment of the children but to textbooks and other planned lesson materials that you can purchase for them. (The Latin plural is *curricula;* English plural is *curriculums.*)

Where Curriculums Come From

Walk into the vendor area of a homeschool convention and you are overwhelmed with scores of booths offering books and videos and all kinds of teaching materials. Open a homeschool catalog and see the same thing. Your problems are 1) trying to look at everything (don't), and 2) trying to choose among them (this chapter should help).

Homeschoolers in the early days, about 1980, had neither of those problems. Their problem was that they could hardly find books. Parents tried to buy Christian school textbooks and found that difficult. The schools and publishers were reluctant to let out teacher's manuals to the general public. The schools feared that their program would be messed up if a pupil got hold of the answer book, or if a parent got hold of it. How was a mere parent to be trusted with a teacher manual? In time, the Christian textbook publishers saw that homeschoolers were a new market for them, and they made the books available even though they were planned for classrooms and not for family learning.

Creative pioneer homeschoolers met their set of problems in numerous ways. Some families managed OK with the classroom-style books, and others began planning materials to fit better. They shared copies with others. Then they printed and sold copies. Thus arose a new breed of publishers, a breed that understood family learning and that produced specifically Christian materials. These "ministry" curriculums were a giant step forward.

These curriculum developers were not hampered by political pressure groups removing too many views, and not burdened with too much committee input. And they were not driven by anti-Bible attitudes. They could be distinctly Christian. In U.S. history in particular they revived much lost history. Admittedly, some few ministry curriculums are poor quality, but many are good.

While the new movement of ministry publishers grew, some Christian businessmen found a way to move into the market quickly. They bought the copyrights to outdated sets of secular workbooks, cleaned out a few references to smoking and such, and called it Christian curriculum. Thus their "Christian homeschool curriculum" was really the old public school curriculum with a shiny face. These same workbooks are now sold under several names, including online versions, and each is promoted as a distinctive type of education. Today's salesmen in those companies may not even know this origin of their curriculum.

Classroom practice in many Christian schools had been to put sixth grade curriculum into fifth grade, fifth grade into fourth, and so on. They believed that if they poured information into children a year earlier they will be a year advanced compared with public schoolers. These books, then, were sold to homeschoolers with the same advanced grade-level designations. Many homeschoolers found the books difficult for their children and, not knowing that the grade level was too high, became discouraged. They blamed themselves or their children rather than the materials.

Major secular booksellers have now moved into the homeschool field in a big way, and they are experienced at advertising and marketing, so they pull in a lot of unwary Christian customers to their secular materials. Your Christian views probably are a major reason that you homeschool, so you should make a point of choosing Christian materials whenever possible. You need also be wary of how the public schools now lure you back to secularism with offer of free books and other help if you sign up for a charter school or other arrangement.

This brief history of homeschool curriculum may help you understand more about the books you see offered.

Labels

The preceding history showed types of publishers: secular and Christian, businessman and ministry. We could add classroom style materials and family style, and we could add professional and amateur. With all those people writing and advertising, it is not surprising to find too many choices out there.

No set of curriculum materials makes a total education system. They contain only academic content, and even that is not tailor-made for your children. They do not meet the heart and soul needs of children as parents can. You constantly are pondering psychological matters such as readiness, interest, and ability to study a particular format. And you almost intuitively judge whether the lessons fit into your biblical philosophy of life. That psychology and philosophy are major underlying components of education, and curriculum content sits on top of those. This puts curriculum in perspective. It is not the driving force of your homeschooling; it is more like a servant. Here is a run-through of various types of curriculum materials that are often used to categorize and to label a homeschool.

The best-known curriculum materials are **textbooks**. In textbooks somebody else besides you has preplanned all the bits of information and spread them out into a specific order to pour into your child's head. Some books do encourage children to think and explore on their own, but this description will do as a one-sentence comparison with other materials. Newer versions of this preplanned curriculum are on electronic media, but they remain the same linear arrangement and separate-subject arrangement as the textbooks or workbooks. Beginning homeschoolers often like to use textbooks because they are familiar and they simplify preparation and planning. Later, most families branch out into more variety, choosing their own books and content.

Using **unit plans** and using **real books** are popular ways to get more variety. A unit means learning about a topic and integrating into it several typical school subjects. For instance, if you study your local water system, that could include geography, science, government, and possibly other school subjects, as well as many language skills. You need not use units totally. You can try a unit now and then, or you can use them most of the time. Publisher planned units are available, but homemade units are surprisingly easy to do, and can be started by just locating a couple of books on a topic you wish to learn more about. Some suppliers help by pre-selecting books for various periods or places in history.

Some other materials are labeled the **principle approach** wherein the authors include content that teaches their particular handpicked principles, mostly having to do with the Christian foundations of America. This, along with others, was labeled also a **notebook approach** because children were instructed to keep a notebook.

Charlotte Mason was a fine educator a century ago and some of her ideas are popularized today, particularly **narrating** books and taking nature walks. Mason dealt mostly with school children and their teachers, but she urged parents to take nature walks with children after their school day. And she urged reading real books, which she called "living books," both at home and at school. You can adopt any Mason ideas, but that does not put you in a box as being a "Mason homeschooler." If you are looking for a full curriculum to follow, some of today's unit materials or textbooks come closer to being complete for your homeschool.

Another label that publishers tried is **mastery learning**. That was a classroom approach wherein the teacher taught and re-taught until every child in the class learned some particular goals. It worked against individualizing, because it tended to hold back the faster learners. It also tended toward a view of learning that fact items are set in a line to be learned and tested, and it worked against the view that children's learning branches out in many ways like a tree. Nevertheless, the label sounded great and some publishers tried promoting their materials to homeschoolers as mastery learning. This seemed not to go over well, and that label is not seen so much these days.

A lot of labels come from forceful advertising. In the early days—the 1980s—there were the textbook system and workbook system. Then a company came along and made the worktext system and, believe it or not, magazine writers and others treated those as three different styles of homeschooling. How much text does a book need to qualify it as a worktext rather than a workbook? Advertisers are clever at inventing catchy words like that. When you look at some of these labels you see the absurdity of classifying your schooling in these ways: textbook, workbook, worktext, notebook, living books, real books. Even drawing a line between units and books is not possible because many books suggest accompanying activities and units always suggest books. Materials themselves overlap into different categories, and users can make them overlap even more.

Homeschoolers have plenty of common sense and those trivial differences in the materials do not define what kind of homeschool you are operating. There is now a wide variety of materials and all can be used in a variety of ways. It is useless to try to categorize them into different types of education—or different styles, or approaches, or whatever term is currently fashionable.

If you choose various materials and various methods, then the labeling people call you eclectic—an education jargon that means you mix systems. But no, you are not mixing systems, simply choosing materials as you wish, to fit into your system, which is called Christian education or Christian homeschooling. That is a comprehensive, unified view of education. Sets of books or unit plans are not that comprehensive; they simply are tools to help.

A popular label today that must be explained more fully is **classical**, which means different things to its different writers and promoters, though they all try in some way to re-create an ancient system of education. This began in modern times with an essay called "The Lost Tools of Learning" by writer Dorothy Sayers. She was a specialist on the Middle Ages and wanted to bring back the good thinking skills of those times. In her essay she used the three Greek words for language learning—*grammar, dialectic,* and *rhetoric.* The classical Greeks had no "science" of grammar; what they called grammar we call literature. By the Roman Middle Ages, children began in primary school, where they learned to read and write, beginning with letters and syllables, and followed by copying one- or two-line pagan moral sayings. Next came secondary school where students did learn grammar as we understand the term today, but they mainly learned the great authors and poets (also pagan). And finally, came higher education where students practiced rhetoric—learning the elegance of an orator.

Sayers' use of the words *grammar, dialectic,* and *rhetoric* differs considerably from ancient use and practice. She applied the words to her invention of three "stages" of child development, and it is these Sayers stages that have spread among homeschoolers as "classical education." It begins in the first stage with memorizing a lot of fact-level information without regard to understanding it.

The more genuine classical education in America was popularized by philosopher Mortimer Adler and came into use mostly by Catholics and mostly at university level. For this education, Adler compiled the original list of Great Books of Western Civilization, which was published by Encyclopedia Britannica in 1952. That list contained parts of the Bible. Their revised list in 1999 contains no Bible, although it includes Augustine, Aquinas, Calvin, and some other Christians. Other people make their own lists to include books of eastern civilizations with their religions, or to include modern books, or in other ways to better fit their education goals.

Adler's belief was that the big ideas that men should contemplate and know in order to be educated are the same for all mankind, in any generation. That is the "perennialist" philosophy of education. Christians, of course, have their own perennialist view that the Bible is what all people should contemplate and know in order to be educated.

With the rich choice of materials out there, you need not label your school according to publishers or sets of books or persons, as Mason or Sayers. You can tell people what materials you are using, but when they ask what kind of homeschool you have, the answer is that you operate a Christian homeschool. That is unified from its foundations on up.

Language Skills versus Content Subjects

It helps in selecting school materials to think of two categories of learning: 1) content subjects and 2) language skills. The language skills include reading, writing, speaking, thinking, and related skills. These are not truly *subjects* for the most part. They are skills you use to learn the subjects. The skill of reading helps students to learn history or science or geography. They can read this content, but they cannot read reading. It is too artificial to teach one by one the little skills of reading. That is, it is artificial to isolate them in a "reading course" instead of helping children to use the skills in their various content subjects.

The schooling industry has isolated reading. It has broken the skill into little pieces, distributed them through the grades, tested at every bend in the road, and at the end of the journey the pieces do not add up to the whole and do not produce lifelong readers. Students can finish the journey and think they have "done" reading in the sense they have done Algebra I.

By contrast, many homeschoolers have learned to treat reading as a skill. Children use it almost from the beginning to read storybooks, dinosaur books, biographies, science—all kinds of content. It turns out that they gain all the little skills that reading textbooks want to teach them, and they gain them in greater measure. Their vocabulary and knowledge and thinking skills grow faster. We do not look for them to end up as readers; they already are readers. Homeschoolers excel in large part because of this view of reading.

Not as many homeschoolers view writing the same way, but they should. Writing, too, is a skill. Children can write all kinds of content but they do not write writing. Similar to reading, there is little need for workbooks or other grade-by-grade materials to specifically teach writing, speaking, thinking, and related language skills. Students should practice these, instead, in all content subjects.

Ancient Languages

Homeschoolers commonly ask about teaching Latin and Greek languages. In the early days of America they had Latin grammar schools where students learned both Latin and Greek so they could read Plato and Cicero and other ancients. Once they could read those languages, they qualified for college. Their math level might have been equivalent to our fifth grade arithmetic, and they probably had no science at all, but they qualified for college entrance.

Nowadays we have all the available Latin and Greek writings in English translation, so students can read them without first spending years learning the languages. Latin is useful for people going into medicine and some other sciences, and it helps bring a deeper understanding of English because it is one of the feeder languages into English. And some few scholars may want to study the ancient manuscripts for themselves. Aside from those uses, Latin does not rate a major place in the education of every child but is a choice for certain people. If your family is not interested in Latin, heave a sigh of relief and move on to something you like better.

As for Greek language, the classical Greek of Plato and the philosophers was several centuries before New Testament times. Christian homeschoolers today would do better to study the Greek of the New Testament, called koine Greek, if they study Greek at all. A shortcut to obtaining ancient language help for English is to study some of the common Greek and Latin word roots and affixes that survive in English. Lists of these are easy to find on the Internet.

Hebrew of the Old Testament is another ancient language to consider, especially for students who intend to pursue biblical studies. Some linguists believe the one language before Babel was the original Hebrew.

Shopping for Curriculum

Many new homeschoolers, and older ones too, buy too much curriculum and then cry for help. They worry about "gaps," about not covering everything. It is a myth that there is an "everything" standard that we all should know. Graduates who are good thinkers can later learn whatever they need. One whole generation had to learn computers on their own. Schools like Massachusetts Institute of Technology hired self-taught men to teach computer until they could raise degreed computer professors. Who knows what your children may need to learn in the future? There is no way to "cover" everything. Aim, instead, to teach your children how to think and learn in whatever content you are using.

The guidelines below should simplify your curriculum shopping and your planning and scheduling as well. You will notice that fewer books are suggested for the language skills and more for the content subjects. Topics here are most of the major subjects and some often-asked-about subjects. They are in alphabetical order.

Arithmetic. For kindergartners you do not need arithmetic books at all. *The Three R's*[1] tells how to give children a stronger arithmetic foundation using real objects and a hundred chart, up to third grade if you can stick with the system that long. Good arithmetic curriculums for these ages try to teach young children with real objects, but that is hard to do in books. Books either tell you to get blocks and things, or they draw pictures of blocks and things, which is not as good as using real toys—and candy and plates and forks.

Arithmetic curriculums have persisted longer than other subjects in following a traditional school approach. But now even arithmetic and higher math are bursting out with creative books that give human meaning and life uses for all those abstract number operations. At least one Web site is keeping up-to-date with these new offerings.[2]

If you want to use the traditional, there are two basic kinds to choose from. The best kind does more to help children understand the number concepts as they go along. The other kind has children simply learn to calculate. They must memorize $5 + 3 = 8$ even if they do not visualize a group of 5, and do not understand that they can count forward 3 to get the answer. You can recognize these books by the large amounts of drill and memorization in them. Some children like this kind because they understand what's going on even without a lot of explanation and manipulatives. One boy liked this drill kind so well that his mom switched his brother to it also. But that did not work, and he had to return to the "understanding" kind. You and your child together might decide what curriculum to buy.

Even at high school algebra and geometry and beyond, some curriculums do better at helping students understand, while others mostly teach rules for calculation and drill on using those rules. College bound students need whatever math their college requires. These students mostly can learn independently, so you do not need to become a math teacher. In some cases you may wish to use an online course or other arrangement that provides teacher help. Those naturally are more expensive. All students, to earn a diploma, need to meet math requirements in their state. Students not talented or proficient in math will likely learn more from the new creative books. You could use some of these and if the children do not do algebra or geometry level math, label a course "general math" on the transcript.

Bible. The main textbook that ties everything together is the Bible. You can begin with Bible storybooks for young children, but phase into the Bible itself. The King James is best for memorizing and for study of important Bible words and concepts.[3] For a powerful study help, obtain the Online Bible.[4]

Computers. In today's world, computers rate alongside books as part of most people's curriculum, so we mention them here. At used computer stores you can find what you want for very little cost. Usually these businesses will also provide help with obtaining and installing second-hand programs and helping you get started. The reason the cost is so low is that many people are constantly upgrading to the newest models and they need something to do with their old. They are not allowed to place them in the trash. So if you are satisfied with less than the latest, you can pick up the discards. Sometimes friends will even give you theirs free. If you buy new, it soon is going to be less than new, anyway. If you know nothing about computers, find a friend in your church or support group to help you shop. Public libraries often provide free classes on computer use.

If you recognize that a computer need not be a major expense, that can help you pass up the public school offer of a free computer if you only buckle under in various ways to the government curriculum. That is important if you want a true Christian education.

Foreign languages. Modern language curriculums are better than a generation ago because they simulate the natural way that children learned their native tongue. That is, they hear it and speak it, learning vocabulary just as two- and three-year-olds learn English. Then they move on to reading and writing the language. The old way was to learn its grammar rules almost from day one and to memorize lists of words each day.

Audio materials for language learning are another advantage today. This helps for pronouncing correctly, and hearing the language adds a rich dimension that was missing in the old textbook system. Language audios could be a way to use some of your car time.

A little known fact is that children up to about age seven can pronounce any sound in any language. Then they lose sounds that they do not use in the language they speak. If you can figure a way to keep alive those sounds, children will be better speakers of any language they later learn. One company prepared for this purpose an audio of simple verses, nursery rhyme pattern. Apparently not enough customers realized the value of this and the ads are no longer found in homeschool magazines.

Grammar. If you teach grammar at all in elementary grades, find one simple book and use it in all the grades. Use it for reference and for an occasional lesson if you want. Alternatively, the grammar you remember from school should be enough to help children with their writing. Skip grammar workbooks. For a teen-level grammar book, get any clearly organized college English handbook. Some homeschool publishers and suppliers offer this one-book system. You could also try Amazon or a college bookstore. Reference books like this help more than grade-by-grade grammar courses.

History and social studies. For history use real books not textbooks. Librarians have learned that textbooks are too expensive, and they can get the same information in real books. Teachers have learned that textbooks are dull, and they can get interesting information in real books. The textbook was a classroom format, so textbooks often come with teacher's edition, student textbook, student workbook, tests, and answer keys. This drives the cost way up there—all for dull history.

School textbooks now water down and rewrite American history much as the Soviets did in their days of power. As a homeschooler you can use books by writers like Peter Marshall, Gary DeMar, Rousas John Rushdoony, Cleon Skousen, William Federer, and newer Christian writers coming along. These offer a good education in history and related social studies. A classic little book that everybody should read is *The Law*[5] written by Frederic Bastiat in 1850. Richard Maybury's books cleverly teach on a child level some important American and capitalist concepts. Such real books are so nutritious for the mind that you probably will want to read them as a family, maybe aloud, so you can feast along with the children.

For books on ancient history, we are in a time of transition. The dates and events have been incorrect in books for the past century. Today, some "revisionists" are discovering how to straighten out many of the errors, but schoolbooks will be the last to switch over to the better history. A number of Christian books do begin with creation and the Flood. Then if they cover much from the Flood to the Greeks, they do not use the revisionist history in that time period. A book that explains all this is *World History Made Simple: Matching History with the Bible*.[6]

Companies that pre-select real books for you outline their history plans in chronological order, but it makes no difference to your children's learning if you change that order. You can read about Pilgrims and some American history before reading about Egypt. Older students have no problem understanding that Egypt is more ancient, and younger children have no concept of such long time frames anyway. All their stories can just be "long ago and far away,"

"Of making many books there is no end" (from Ecclesiastes 12:12). This probably is truer in history than in any subject. All your children can find much to interest them among the real books that homeschool suppliers offer.

Music. Today, there are many kinds of self-teaching piano materials. It is not necessary to take children to a teacher for piano or to take your dog to a class for obedience. Try both at home like everything else. Piano is advantageous for all music students to study for a while because the keys are good visual aids. You see what you are doing when you play a C chord, whereas you miss the visual with a guitar. Many guitarists end up knowing next to nothing about music theory and music reading if they learn only guitar. Learning piano helps with all other instruments.

You can find self-teaching books for whatever instrument your children may want. Use them, but use piano too. More books today teach chords early on and children can play satisfying songs after only a few lessons. Older books took the slow approach of first learning all the details of reading and naming notes, counting time, and fingering precisely, so that enjoying music almost got lost in the process. You can use teachers later on for children who want it. Also join orchestra and choir groups when available. Music is a group activity more than most subjects.

Penmanship. At first while children are learning how to form the letters, you can buy or make a wall chart or desk chart of letters to use at least until about third grade when children are proficient in writing manuscript. Then get a chart for cursive writing. At first, write family names and other single words, then move on to sentences to practice the skill of penmanship. You could also use a curriculum for a while if you like, but children certainly do not need six years of penmanship bookwork to practice writing. That is a holdover from the nineteenth century when handwriting was an essential business skill. Today there is more need to learn good keyboard skills for business.

After children learn to write, instead of every-day, every-year penmanship practice try a "crash course" targeted to their particular problems. Two methods for this are copying models of letters that you select, and practicing rhythm. These are described briefly in the writing chapter here and more fully in *You Can Teach Your Child Successfully*.[7]

Phonics. Many phonics programs are overkill. They are like teachers' college level, or even the linguist level, teaching what the whole phonics system is—every sound, their many spellings, their categories, linguistic terms and definitions, and oodles of rules (with many exceptions). If you do not know all this but you read anyway, consider that your children could read too while being less than experts on the phonics system. Reading practice builds up facility in *using* phonics, and that is what matters.

Susannah Wesley taught her nine living children to read without benefit of a complex phonics kit and even without beginning reading textbooks. You could, too, with the vast majority of children. If you do buy a phonics program, look for something simple and inexpensive. If you do not start too early with your children, they will learn all the phonics they need in a few months.

Reading. Pass by reading textbooks altogether, certainly for children who can read a little bit. Children can learn to read without textbooks at all, with only children's storybooks.[8] Before textbook days, parents used the Bible. You know what the letters sound like. You know the words *the* and *one* that do not sound out easily, so you can tell children. Bit by bit and patiently tuning in to the child's pace and his teachable moments will take 90 percent of children through the beginning stages of reading. (For the other 10 percent, see the Appendix.)

In case you do want beginning reading materials, know that the kinds that work fastest are those that teach a few sounds and then provide reading practice with those sounds. Instant reading. Then they move on to more sounds and more reading. Homeschoolers call these "phonics readers." After children read enough to read children's books, you can drop the reading course. Let them read dinosaur books or whatever they like. This will expand their reading vocabulary faster than textbooks would. The texts actually slow down progress, because they confine the vocabulary to "grade level" words and because they have only short reading passages and perhaps one workbook page per day.

Science. Homeschool catalogs these days are burgeoning with science books and materials of all kinds, many of them from Christian publishers. Materials from Answers in Genesis (AIG) and Institute for Creation Research (ICR) contain excellent science teaching and are widely available.[9] The children's magazine from AIG can almost be a complete science curriculum, with surprises every quarter. With all this choice there is no need to select items with an evolutionary bias. Students who read books and magazines from creation scientists gain plenty of practice in thinking critically about science—both evolutionary and biblical science. They also gain the vocabulary they need for reading and understanding in many fields of science.

For students who want to *do* something in science, they can obtain kits and equipment from several homeschool suppliers, and they can use real life. Cleaning fish or helping a hunter clean his deer can certainly substitute for the common lab exercise of dissecting a frog. Some children (future surgeons?) actually love to kill a snake and skin it, or dissect other unfortunate creatures. Kitchen and garage activities often involve science matters too.

For students who prefer defined courses, you could use published ones or plan your own with the easy planning method of listing some topics to study. Find topic ideas in a borrowed textbook or on the Internet, where your state probably has lists. The student can record his time and activities, trying to count up about 150 hours of reading, writing, and experiences for a credit on the transcript. This after-the-fact system is easier than trying to plan all details ahead of time.

Students who liked free reading in the lower grades could continue that in high school. Everybody does not need hands-on science, but they all need minds-on. Since the public school approach to science has not shown itself to be the best, you need not use that as a model. Use any of the homeschool materials that your students prefer. With commitment they can achieve high in science.

Spelling. Spelling curriculums ordinarily are a waste of time. Why have your children study twenty words per week that somebody else selected? Most homeschoolers who try this soon discover that children may score 100 on a Friday test but then miss the same words while writing the following week. Take advice from those families and do not buy that kind of curriculum.

The main goals for spelling are to instill an attitude that spelling matters and to train habits of finding and using correct spelling. For specific spelling lessons, use words that your children miss in their writing. If you buy any spelling books at all, the best kind is one that gives ideas for individualizing spelling to each child. One book will do for all the grades. Other single-book systems have phonetic spelling help or give the 5000 most common words. Use parts of such a single book when and where you want and save it for a reference. That way, the items your children studied are available for reference and review and not lost in a pile of used workbooks.

Vocabulary. Integrate vocabulary learning in all subjects and do not bother with separate vocabulary curriculum. Children learn thousands of words per year while they are still preschoolers, and you never use a lesson or curriculum for that. The same efficient system of vocabulary building continues as children read widely. Converse with them about their science and history and fiction books. Unit plans often give ideas for writing about history and other subjects. These *uses* of the words in listening, reading, and writing build vocabulary the natural way. Weekly vocabulary lessons work like traditional spelling lessons. That is, the out-of-context words may be forgotten the week after passing a test on them.

A useful kind of vocabulary study is to learn about Greek and Latin roots and affixes in our English words. Find this information on the Internet or in a one-book style that some homeschool suppliers offer.

Worldview. Think Biblically edited by John MacArthur describes worldviews directly as they come from the Bible.[10] Some other worldview books are heavy with philosophy, teaching various views and what is wrong with them, and students who like reading philosophy may enjoy these.

Writing. As described in the writing chapter, writing is a language skill and not primarily a content subject, so the best procedure is for children to practice writing in other subjects or in real-life situations rather than adding an extra subject called writing or composition. If you want writing curriculums at some points in your children's schooling, look for those that teach mostly matters of good style rather than emphasizing grammar rules.

Teens who already write rather well can profit from books on writing style. Some will be permanent books that deserve a place alongside the grammar reference and the dictionary. One kind of stylebook is the reference like the *Chicago Manual of Style.* The other kind is what you actually read, like the popular little book by Strunk and White, *The Elements of Style.* Many homeschool suppliers carry this. Find others by searching www.Amazon.com for books on writing style. Some teenagers enjoy reading in these books. For those who don't read them on their own, you might assign selected parts now and then.

Money-Saving Tip

After you write out a list of materials to order, set it aside for a while. When you get it out again, you probably will immediately decide on some items to delete from the list. For the rest, choose some to order immediately and some to delay. As schooling proceeds you will be able to make better decisions on the delay list.

Scheduling

Homeschool scheduling is much simplified once you think of the language skills as different from the content subjects. You now do not need six or more "classes" per day: arithmetic, reading, spelling, writing, history, geography, and more.

A high school girl became involved in debating. She and a friend formed a team and entered the homeschool debating tournaments going all the way to the nationals. Her mother said, "Katie doesn't need any other curriculum except math." The numerous language skills included reading, taking notes, organizing and writing out arguments, listening to and taking notes on other debaters, conversing and working closely with her teammate, thinking and solving problems, and of course speaking. The debate topic that year, as usual, was how to solve a particular worldwide problem. This included the content subjects of science, geography, governments, international relations, and some history. All this was in a highly charged motivating atmosphere. You could add the social skills of working with a teammate and relating well with competitors and judges. If there was anything to worry about, it might be that Katie spent too much time studying.

Compare this with the usual school schedule of one hour of government, one hour of speech, and so on through a high school day, and you get a good picture of the artificiality of schooling. To make a transcript in cases like Katie's it may be difficult to count up clock hours to turn into credits. Instead, you could decide that the writing surely fulfills a course in English composition, and proceed in this manner to fill out a transcript.

In elementary grades you can similarly break down the artificial school structures. Center your efforts on providing a rich education in the content subjects, and even those do not need to be scheduled daily—a history period, a geography period, a science period, a music period, and so forth. If a science interest gobbles up too much of a child's time, make a mental note to have some good history books ready for when the science interest wanes or is finished.

If a child's learning is not that self-propelling yet, you can work more on scheduling and building study habits. Start the day with reading and memorizing the Bible. Follow with arithmetic. If possible spend some time sitting beside the child and let him explain to you what he is doing. Or you explain what he needs to do. That's called tutoring, and it is a powerful method of teaching. Schedule time for reading—any and everything, including fiction.

Read some things aloud as a family. Children can read others independently. Help them notice new words and make lists or cards to review or to use while writing. If you are reading about space travel, for instance, you may collect words like astronaut, orbit, cosmic radiation, and zero gravity. Place the list in plain view on a wall and the children can refer to it when they write about space travel. Routines like this take the place of separate classes for spelling, vocabulary, and English composition. You strengthen the science learning and get some writing and spelling practice at the same time.

Published curriculum materials should not drive your Christian homeschool. You sit in the driver's seat, so do not fret about keeping up with schedules and sequence formulas in the books. Each child is unique. Teach the child and not the book. The one unchanging Book can guide your curriculum choices as it guides everything else in your life.

Remember that you are not alone sequestered within your four walls. You are part of a vibrant movement of millions that already has made a big difference and that will make even more in the days we have remaining before Christ returns.

APPENDIX:

CROSSED-DOMINANCE PROBLEMS

The problem of crossed dominance or mixed dominance affects approximately 10 percent of children. This term means that a child is not completely right or left sided. Ideally hand, foot, eye, and ear should all match as either right or left dominant.

Some symptoms of this dominance problem include confusing *b* and *d* or *was* and *saw*, squinting eyes, or difficulty giving attention to close work. Do not panic the first time a child confuses *b* with *d*. All children need to learn that letters are not like a fork, which is still a fork no matter which way you turn it. But if the reversals persist after careful teaching, and if the child is older than six or so, then you could pursue a diagnosis. Do not worry before that age because sidedness is normally not settled until about age five. And do not force right-handedness (or left) before that time. Let children take all the time they need to develop neurologically.

Infants, too, need to develop in the normal way. One infant lived in Nome, Alaska. He was never allowed on the cold floor and spent most of his time in a high chair or a small playpen. By third grade he experienced serious reading problems. He cured this, as explained below, by practicing the crawling that he had missed. Do not rush children at any growth stage. They need normal crawling and other body movements for proper brain and neurological development.

High fever, lack of oxygen, and other physical trauma to the body also affect early development. In practically all these cases where the problems are caused during children's development, they can be "cured" as described below. God created us with amazing over-design in the brain and other systems, so we can train the body to learn what it missed in the early years.

Diagnosis. Here are some informal diagnostic tests that require no special equipment.

1. To check **eye**, roll a sheet of paper and have the child hold the tube at arm's length and look through it at your nose. Which eye of the child's do you see through the tube? In practically all cases that is his dominant eye (see Figure 1).

Figure 1. Sighting

2. To check **foot**, roll a ball toward the child and ask him to kick it back to you. Repeat this several times trying to roll exactly to center position, so as not to get a false result because the ball rolls too far left or right. An alternative is to hand the child a ball and ask him to kick it to you.

3. To check **ear**, have the child sit in a chair and from behind slowly move a ticking watch or timer first toward one side and then toward the other. Ask the child to signal as soon as he hears the ticking. Determine which ear hears at the farthest distance.

4. To check **hand**, observe which hand the child normally uses for eating, drawing, throwing a ball and other activities.

The last test, handedness, is the most tricky of all these. If you find, for instance, that the child uses his right hand for coloring and the left for eating, then search into his history. Was he started on workbooks or close paperwork before age five and encouraged to use his right hand? If so, that left-handed eating might be a hint that he was born to be left handed but was trained to use his right hand for certain activities and now exhibits a mixed dominance. In such a case it may take only a few days or weeks to retrain the left hand to write.

If the eye is out of line with the rest of the body, then vision therapy can help. This takes a doctor rarer than the usual optometrist or ophthalmologist who checks acuity—the 20/20 scores. Vision therapists may bill themselves as such, but the Yellow Pages often do not list them that way. These days there is usually someone in each support group or at least in the office of the state homeschool organization who can direct you to one of these therapists. Try to find one who will give you exercises to work on at home instead of doing everything in his office, which will cost more than it needs to.

If the ear is out of line, that is less likely to cause reading problems, but it brings other symptoms. For instance, a child may listen to your directions or assignment and then look intently at you for a time before responding. During that time he is repeating the words to himself—moving them to the other side of his brain. Then he understands them.

Mixed dominance causes reading problems because any sensory message from the right side of the body goes to the left side of the brain and vice versa. Thus if a child is writing with his right hand, that kinesthetic message goes to the left side of his brain. And if his dominant left eye is following the writing, that visual message goes to the right side of the brain. Then the brain has to "stutter" a bit to get the two messages together, and it may settle for seeing the *b* as a *d*.

Treatment. Fortunately, in most cases you can cure this problem by using cross-pattern exercises described below that help to retrain the neurological system. Some parents have found that therapists and specialists charge a high hourly rate for doing these very same exercises.

1. *Cross-pattern crawling* (see Figure 2). On hands and knees, place right hand forward and left knee forward. Then slide left hand and right knee simultaneously until they are forward. Turn head to look at the forward hand. If this is difficult, you need to get beside the child and help him position correctly after each step. Practice a few minutes each day until the child can crawl rhythmically by himself in this cross-pattern fashion. Three or four weeks should bring excellent results.

2. *Cross-pattern walking* (see Figure 3). Stand with left foot forward, right hand pointing downward at the left foot. Turn head slightly to look directly at the forward

Figure 2. Cross-pattern crawling

foot. When ready, step forward with the right foot, left hand pointing and head turning to the right foot. Again, help as much as needed to get the child into the correct position after each step. Practice each day until the child does this easily and rhythmically.

3. *Cross-pattern "swimming."* Lie on stomach with face turned to the left. Bend left elbow so hand is close to face. Bend left knee and bring it up close to elbow. Stretch right arm and leg straight downward. Count one, two, three, turn. On the word *turn* reverse the position; turn face to right, bend right arm and leg and straighten left arm and leg. Help the child get everything in position and count again. Practice a few minutes each day. By about three weeks the child should be able to do this smoothly and rhythmically, and faster than at first. (These positions are the same as the sleep positions shown in Figures 4 and 5.)

Figure 3. Cross-pattern walking

4. *Sleep position* (Figures 4 and 5). Learn to sleep in the
   positions described in exercise 3 on the previous page
   Right-handers sleep lying on the right side of head, face
   turned left, left arm and leg bent, right arm and leg
   downward. Left-handers sleep in the opposite position.

These exercises are in themselves a diagnostic procedure. If a
child has no trouble performing these, then this mixed or crossed
dominance is not a problem with him. This method was originated

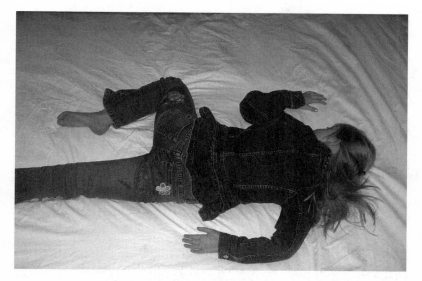

Figure 4. Right-sided sleep pattern

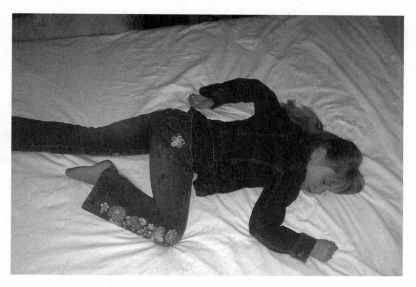

Figure 5. Left-sided pattern

by Dr. Carl Delacato in the 1950s. It became popular and proved to be highly effective, so effective that it is not a stretch to say that children were "cured" of their problem. Today some books and workshops present other methods that seem to show success too.

Some few children with mixed dominance, about 10 percent, have inherited the condition. These conditions will not correct, as the developmental problems do. Explain to these children as much as you can about their situation. This frees them from feeling that they are dumb or do not work hard enough or something that is their fault. Tell them that they can learn to read but will have to work harder than other children. Use kinesthetic methods during the phonics stage of reading. Read to them materials they cannot read for themselves. These students often study engineering or other fields that do not require much reading. And they might excel at piano or become switch hitters in baseball. God has a plan for each life.

Checklist for Left-Right Dominance

Eye: left _____ right _____ not sure _____

Foot: left _____ right _____ not sure _____

Ear: left _____ right _____ not sure _____

Hand: left _____ right _____ not sure _____

Checklist for Dominance Exercises

Cross-pattern crawling:

      needs work _____ does well _____

Cross-pattern walking:

      needs work _____ does well _____

Cross-pattern swimming:

      needs work _____ does well _____

Sleep position:

      forgets _____ often uses it _____

NOTES

CHAPTER 1

1. E. D. Hirsch Jr., et al, *The Dictionary of Cultural Literacy* (Boston: Houghton Mifflin, 1988), 1. The later grade-by-grade versions of this made for public schools omit all the Bible items that were in the original research data.

2. Northrup Frye, *The Educated Imagination* (Bloomington, IN: Indiana University Press, 1974), xviii.

3. Download the Online Bible program from www.onlinebibleUSA. com. Order the CD by phone (afternoons) 519-664-2266, or mail Larry Pierce, 11 Holmwood Street, Winterbourne ONT, N0B 2V0, Canada. Available in Windows format and also an easy-to-use DOS format. Another free program is e-Sword at www.e-sword.net.

4. Northrup Frye, *The Great Code: The Bible and Literature* (New York, Harcourt Brace Jovanovich, 1982), 29.

5. Ibid. 81.

6. Ruth Beechick, *Children's Understanding of Parables: A Developmental Study* (Tempe, AZ: Arizona State University, 1974).

7. See *One Book Stands Alone* by Dr. Douglas D. Stauffer (Milbrook, AL: McCowen Mills Publishers, 2001). This is a very readable book about differences between the King James Bible and the newer English versions. From among hundreds of examples in this book, here are a few salvation verses either missing or changed in the new versions: Matthew 18:11, Luke 9:56, John 6:47, Acts 8:37, and Ephesians 1:13.

CHAPTER 2

1. *Adam and His Kin* by Ruth Beechick (1990) is an eye-opening narrative of the Genesis 1 to 11 period for age ten and up. *Genesis: Finding Our Roots,*

also by Beechick (1997), is an in-depth study of the same period for teens. To order go to www.MottMedia.com or call 800-421-6645.

2. Answers in Genesis offers inexpensive models of the Ark to make in two sizes. To order to go www.AnswersBookstore.com or call 800-778-3390.

3. See Genesis 13:10, which says that Egypt was as the garden of the Lord *before* God destroyed Sodom and Gomorrah, and verse 19:24, which says He rained brimstone and fire from heaven.

4. See 1 Samuel 15:1–8, which tells that Saul destroyed the Amalekites from Shur, a part of Egypt where they had their capital city. (Some translations sound as if the Amalekites had only one city, but the original says that Saul went to *one of the* cities to meet them in battle.)

5. A Tabernacle Model Kit with a video and workbook are available from www.visionvideo.com or by calling 800-523-0226.

6. Several books show a plan of the Temple. One which compares Solomon's Temple with Ezekiel's vision is *Only Jesus of Nazareth Can Sit on the Throne of David* by John McTernan, an author with longtime federal investigating experience. He uses Ezekiel 40 to 48 to make his airtight case for the Messiah (Oklahoma City: Hearthstone Publishers, 2005).

7. Don DeYoung, PhD, *Thousands not Billions: Challenging an Icon of Evolution* (Green Forest, AR: Master Books, 2005). To order go to www.icr.org or call 619-448-0900.

8. One book that clearly explains all this is *World History Made Simple: Matching History with the Bible* by Ruth Beechick. This several-week unit is for young teens or for whole family use (Fenton MI: MottMedia, 2006). To order go to www.MottMedia.com or call 800-421-6645.

CHAPTER 3

1. Hapgood, Charles, *Maps of the Ancient Sea Kings* (Kempton, IL: Adventures Unlimited Press, 1966).

2. Two major suppliers of education materials with the biblical view of creation and the Flood are: Institute for Creation Research (www.icr.org or 619-448-0900) and Answers in Genesis (www.AnswersInGenesis.org or 859-778-3390). Also see this source of excellent teen science videos: Kent Hovind, 29 Cummings Road, Pensacola FL 32503 (www.drdino.com or 877-479-3466).

CHAPTER 4

1. Interview with John MacArthur by Paul Suarez for *The Old Schoolhouse* magazine, Winter, 2004.

2. John MacArthur, PhD, and faculty of Master's College, *THINK BIBLICALLY: Recovering a Christian Worldview* (Wheaton, IL: Crossway Books, 2003). To order go to www.BooksChristian.com or call 160-682-4300).

3. See "The Biblical Hebrew Creation Account: New Numbers Tell the Story" (#377) by Steven W. Boyd, PhD, available at www.icr.org. Search for the word *poetry* and it will call up this article.

4. See chapter 3 note 2 for some sources of biblical science materials.

5. An excellent book to clarify the place of Islam today is *Judgment Day! Islam, Israel and the Nations* by Dave Hunt (Bend, OR: The Berean Call, 2005).

6. *Learning About Islam* by The Voice of the Martyrs missionary organization (www.persecution.com or 800-747-0085).

CHAPTER 5

1. One possibility is *Finding Financial Freedom: A Biblical Guide to Your Independence* by Grant Jeffrey (New York: WaterBrook Press, a Division of Random House, 2005).

2. Frank Coffield, David Mosely, Elaine Hall, and Kathryn Ecclestone, *Should we be using learning styles? What research has to say to practice* (London: Learning & Skills Research Center, 1989), 52.

3. Full data from research on the word heart in the Bible is included in *Heart and Mind: What the Bible Says about Learning* by Ruth Beechick (Fenton, MI: MottMedia, 2004), 135–72). To order go to www.MottMedia.com or call 800-421-6645.

4. This information comes from award-winning researchers, Drs. John I. and Beatrice C. Lacey. Several of their studies are available on Internet.

5. Examples are given in *The Heart's Code* by Paul Pearsall (New York: Broadway Books, 1998).

6. Reported by Frank Sherwin, MS. For his article, go to www.icr.org and search for the word "larynx."

CHAPTER 6

1. Extensive directions for this kind of beginning reading is given in *Teach a Child to Read with Children's Books* by Mark B. Thogmartin (Bloomington, IN: EDINFO Press, 1996).

Chapter 10

1. Taken from *Teaching Primaries* by Ruth Beechick (Denver, CO: Accent Publications, 1980, or Elgin, IL: David Cook, 1988). English edition now out of print.

Chapter 11

1. Ruth Beechick, *The Three R's* (Fenton MI: MottMedia, 2006). To order go to www.MottMedia.com or call 800-421-6645. This book also tells how and when to start reading and writing.

2. At this writing, www.livingmath.net has a good listing of innovative arithmetic materials.

3. Much information on this is in Stauffer, chapter 1 note 7.

4. See chapter 1 note 3 for online Bible helps.

5. Frederic Bastiat, *The Law,* 1850, translated 1950 by Dean Russell (the Foundation for Economic Education, 1968, and Irving on Hudson, 1998). Some homeschool suppliers carry this. It is also available for download from Internet.

6. Beechick, chapter 2 note 8.

7. Ruth Beechick, *You Can Teach Your Child Successfully* (Fenton MI: MottMedia, 1988). To order go to www.MottMedia.com or call 800-421-6645.

8. This system is popularized again today by Mark B. Thogmartin. In *Teach a Child to Read with Children's Books* this Christian reading specialist familiar with homeschooling gives a list of books to use and numerous suggestions for using them to teach reading, phonics, and writing together. See chapter 6 note 1.

9. See chapter 3 note 2 for how to contact these creation science organizations.

10. MacArthur, chapter 4 note 2.

Index

acrostic 15, 17
Adam 23, 25–26, 62, 74
ADD and ADHD 109
Adler, Mortimer 84, 181
age-day theory 61–62
Alaska 82
Alexander the Great 32
Amalekites 208
Answers in Genesis (AIG) 191, 208
Antarctica 45
AP tests 56
Aristotle 46, 51
arithmetic 80–81, 185

Babel 46, 67, 102
Bacon, Francis 108
Barzun, Jacques 136
Bastiat, Frederic 188
biographies 38, 47, 53
book reports 105
Boyd, Steven W. 63
Bronze Age 35
Bruner, Jerome 161

Caesar Augustus 33
Cambrian 49
carbon dating 64
cartoons 79
church and state 83
Churchill, Winston 148
Cicero 183

classical 70, 180–81
CLEP tests 56
commas 134–35
communism 59, 61, 72–73
community helpers 163
conservation, law of 51
Constantine, Emperor 19
content subjects 1–2, 18, 21, 93,
    182–83, 194–95
conversing 18, 93, 106, 164
Copernicus 46
copying 132–33, 181, 190
couplets 14–17
crash course, penmanship 190
Curie, Marie 42
Curie, Pierre 42
cyclical, history 24
Cyrus 32

Daniel 32–34, 38
death sentence 74–75
deep learning 118
Delacato, Carl 204
DeMar, Gary 188
descriptive essays 142
Dick and Jane readers 96–97, 100
dictation 133, 138
DNA code 63
doctrine 7–11, 21

ear approach 151–52

Ecclesiastes 189
Edison 42
education, public 6, 92
Einstein 42, 51
Encyclopedia Britannica 181
English grammar schools 148
entropy, law of 51
euphemisms 83
Eusebius 19
evolution, biological 49–50, 64
expository essays 141
eye development 172

Federer, William 188
Felder, Richard M. 87
Flesch readability formula 20
foreign languages 162, 187
fossils 49–50, 62
Froebel, Fredrich 160
Frye, Northrup 5, 11–13

Galileo 41, 46
games, for thinking 80–81
gap theory 62
Gardner, Howard 85
Genesis, writers of 25–28
geology 49–50
Goals 2000 41, 43, 56
grammar materials 154–55
graphic organizers 123
graphs 80, 84
Great Books of Western
   Civilization 181
Greece 29, 32–34, 70, 91
Greek, language 15, 19–20, 32,
   128, 148, 181, 183–84, 193
Greeks 32, 44, 65, 70, 84, 86, 91,
   181

Gregorc, Anthony F. 87
guide words 116–18

hand dominance 172
handwriting 5, 121, 133
heart 178, 189–92, 209
Hirsch 5
history 23–40, 46, 70, 147, 176–77,
   187–89
Homer 147
Hort, Fenton J. A. 20
humanism 61, 69
hundred chart 185

Institute for Creation Research,
   The (ICR) 35, 191, 208
Islam 67–69, 71

Jacob 27–28
Jurassic 49

Kepler, Johannes 46, 51
King James translators 19, 127

language skills 1–2, 18, 21,
   182–83, 194–95
Latimer, Lewis 42
Latin grammar schools 148, 183
Latin, language 19, 128, 148–53,
   155, 183–84, 193
Law, The 188
Lazear, David 85
left brain 85, 197–204
linear, history 24
logic 16, 91, 93

MacArthur, John 59–60, 193
Majority Text 20

manipulative art 165
Marshall, Peter 188
Mason, Charlotte 84, 179, 182
Masoretic text 19, 32
Massachusetts Institute
  of Technology 184
Master's College, The 60, 63
mastery learning 179
Maybury, Richard 188
McGuffey, William 96
memorizing 125–29, 169–70
metaphor 12, 16–17
Michener, James A. 143–44
Middle Kingdom, Egypt 26, 29
ministry publishers 43, 176
Monitor and the Merrimac, The 106
Montessori, Maria 160
Moses, books of 25–27, 29, 46
music 85, 112–13, 168–69, 189

narration 63, 107, 179
narrative essays 142
Nebuchadnezzar 32–33
New Age 65–67
New England Primer, The 96
New Kingdom, Egypt 31
Newton, Issac 41, 46
Noah, tomb of 25
nutrition 53, 110, 113, 162

Old Kingdom, Egypt 26, 29
Online Bible 6, 186
Origen 19–20
outlining 123, 137
overthrusts 50
overturnings 50

parables 13, 16

penmanship 133, 189–90
perennialist 181–82
Persia 32, 34
persuasive essays 141–42
phonics 95–101, 159, 161, 165,
  171–72, 190–91, 204
physics 50–51, 78
Plato 70, 183–84
poetry, Hebrew 14–16
possessive case 149–50
prehistoric times 36
prepositions 148, 150
prescriptive approach 151, 155
principle approach 179
Psalms
  23 127–28
  24 16
  34 15
  104 16
  113 15
punctuation 132–34, 136

reading 54–57, 86, 95–109,
  118–24, 165, 171–72, 182–83,
  190–91
  problems 197–204
real books 38, 40, 56–57,
  178–80, 187–89
Received Text 19
Red Sea 29
Renaissance 70
representative art 166–67
right brain 85, 197–204
Roman Empire 33–34
Romans 8–10, 90, 117, 148
Rushdoony, Rousas John 188
Russell, Bertrand 41

safety 162–63
Samuel 71
Satan 8, 24, 48, 68
SAT essays 142–43
Saul 31, 35, 208
Sayers, Dorothy 180–82
schooling, government 6, 39
science 41–58, 61–65, 147, 181–83,
    191–92
self-concept 113
Septuagint 19, 32
Shakespeare 128
Shur 208
signatures, in Genesis books 25–28
Skousen, Cleon 188
Sodom and Gomorrah 208
Solomon 31, 35, 72
speed-reading 104–05
spelling 132–33, 138, 165,
    192, 196
Stevenson, Robert Lewis 145
Stirling, Colonel David 88–89
Stone Age 35
styles 39, 84, 86–89, 180
Sumerians 25, 44–45
summaries, writing of 123–24
surface learning 118

Terman, Lewis 84
textbooks 37, 42–44, 96, 118–21,
    178
Textus Receptus 19–20
theology 7–11, 60
thinking, biblical 41, 70, 91
Thrax, Dionysus 147–48
Three R's, The 185
Trinity 8
typology 12–13

unit studies 37

verb infinitives 148
vitamin C 82–83
vocabulary 18, 57, 103, 143, 159,
    164–65, 171–72, 183, 192–93, 196

Wesley, Susannah 95, 97, 190
Westcott, Brooke 20
whole method, of memorizing
    125–27, 169
who/whom 151–52
Winnie the Pooh 107
World History Made Simple 188
worldview 59–65, 74, 193
writing 193–94
    reinvention of 46
    mechanics of 131–35, 155–56
    style 11–12

Yalta Conference 33
You Can Teach Your Child
    Successfully 190